JACKIE HARDING and LIZ M.

How to make
OBSERVATIONS & ASSESSMENTS

2nd Edition

Hodder & Stoughton

A MEMBER OF THE HODDER HEADLINE GROUP

Orders: please contact Bookpoint Ltd, 130 Milton Park, Abingdon, Oxon OX14 4SB. Telephone: (44) 01235 827720, Fax: (44) 01235 400454. Lines are open from 9.00 - 6.00, Monday to Saturday, with a 24 hour message answering service. Email address: orders@bookpoint.co.uk

British Library Cataloguing in Publication Data
A catalogue record for this title is available from The British Library

ISBN 0 340 78038 X

First published 2000
Impression number   10   9   8   7   6   5   4
Year   2005   2004   2003

Cover photo by Mick Thomas
Typeset by Wearset, Boldon, Tyne and Wear.
Printed for Hodder & Stoughton Educational, a division of Hodder Headline , 338 Euston Road, London NW1 3BH by Oriental Press, Dubai, UAE.

Contents

Acknowledgements

Jackie Harding and Liz Meldon-Smith would like to thank the following individuals and establishments for their valuable contributions to this book: Heath Clark Nursery; Coulsdon Nursery School; Thelma Perkins; Marissa Simmonds; 'High Scope' 190/192 Maple Road, London SE1 8HT; 'Playladders' Hannah Mortimer, Anderby Hall, Northallerton, North Yorkshire DL79 6LU; 'All about me' by S. Wolfendale; Alistair and Hannah Mottram; Charlotte and Ryan Pascal; Frances Hare, Croydon School Advisory Service; Christopher Mark Edwards; Carole Blomstrom; Carolyn Childs; Kimberley Christie-Sturgis for her contributions to some of the photographs in this book; Grenville, Samuel and Hollyanne; Roger, Anna and Naomi; Ben Viret; British Paediatric Association; Margaret Coats; and the Child Care and Education Department at Croydon College for their support and encouragement.

Many of the photographs in this book were taken at Purley Nursery School by Mick Thomas and Wendy Chilton. The authors would like to thank them and the staff for their contribution. The photograph on page 23 (top) is courtesy of the Format Photo Agency.

Introduction

Aims

This book aims to:

- develop your understanding of the reasons for undertaking observations
- develop your confidence as an observer
- help you plan systematically for observation work
- help you identify suitable methods for observing
- encourage you to value observation writing as a lifelong skill
- develop your understanding of how to use assessments in future planning and as a guide to personal learning
- help you develop an understanding of how and when to pass on information gained from observation and assessment
- help you build up a portfolio of evidence for NVQ

■ WHO WILL BENEFIT FROM THIS BOOK?

This book is intended to help all those who are interested in promoting the learning, development and well-being of children under eight years of age according to their individual needs.

The authors do not claim to describe the only or even the best way of doing observations, but this book will help both the novice and the experienced observer look afresh at how they use their skills.

All early years workers whether on a course or in post will benefit from acquiring observation skills. Whether you are a playworker, NVQ candidate, child minder, health visitor, teacher, interested parent or any other worker with children under eight years of age, observation work should partner practice. You are invited to use all or parts of this book depending on your experience.

■ WHAT IS MEANT BY OBSERVATIONS AND ASSESSMENTS?

Observations are close examinations of children, perhaps focusing on their play, language, behaviour or other aspects of development.

Assessments allow you to evaluate what you have seen or heard; these evaluations in turn help you make decisions or *recommendations* about what is best for the children.

National Vocational Qualifications (NVQs): Early Years Care and Education

NVQs are work-based, nationally recognised qualifications. They do not invalidate any current qualifications you may hold. They are complementary. All NVQ training and assessment is validated by one of the nationally approved awarding bodies such as CACHE, Edexcel and City and Guilds and through the Qualifications and Curriculum Authority (QCA).

■ THE 'THINKING ABOUT OBSERVING' CHART

The chart on page vii will help you monitor your progress through this book. It appears at the end of every chapter and you can use it to plan effectively. This will help you learn about the process of observing and assessing.

The chart illustrates the framework of this book. It serves as a guide to how the various elements of the book relate to each other.

■ USING THIS BOOK

- ■ Use the chart at the end of each chapter to review your progress.
- ■ The In-depth discussion boxes may be useful if you are an experienced child care worker and have some knowledge of observations and assessments. These sections are intended to challenge your perceptions, enhance your work with children and consolidate good practice.
- ■ Activity boxes are useful for students and tutors for promoting discussion or drawing out a particular point.
- ■ Helpful hint boxes are used as a way of expressing the authors' own experiences of observing young children.
- ■ Quality control boxes contain suggestions for maintaining a professional outlook whilst carrying out observations and assessments.

■ THINKING ABOUT OBSERVING

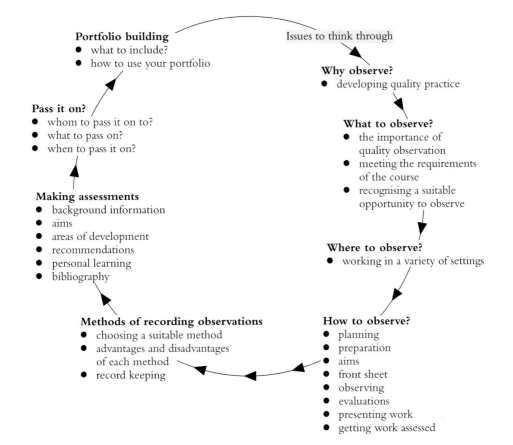

Portfolio building
- what to include?
- how to use your portfolio

Pass it on?
- whom to pass it on to?
- what to pass on?
- when to pass it on?

Making assessments
- background information
- aims
- areas of development
- recommendations
- personal learning
- bibliography

Methods of recording observations
- choosing a suitable method
- advantages and disadvantages of each method
- record keeping

Issues to think through

Why observe?
- developing quality practice

What to observe?
- the importance of quality observation
- meeting the requirements of the course
- recognising a suitable opportunity to observe

Where to observe?
- working in a variety of settings

How to observe?
- planning
- preparation
- aims
- front sheet
- observing
- evaluations
- presenting work
- getting work assessed

1

Thinking about Observing

Aims

In this chapter we aim to:

■ ensure that you understand the basic concepts for observing and assessing

■ help you observe on a daily basis

■ help you learn to be objective in your observations

■ help you think what it feels like to be observed.

■ BASIC CONCEPTS

First you need to consider some important basic concepts. These will help you be successful in your work and ensure that your work reflects good practice.

This might be the first time you have ever thought about observing young children and it might be quite exciting to know that your observations will be totally original! You need never worry that your work differs in detail from someone else's work. No two observations can ever be the same because no two children will ever be the same or act in the same way.

You need to have confidence to record what you see and hear and this will be unique.

Equal opportunities

Child care practice must take into account the child's and family's customs, values and spiritual beliefs. It is essential that a child care worker's practice is anti-discriminatory regarding race, gender, age, class, disability, marital status, sexual orientation and religion. At all times guard against racist and sexist attitudes.

You are less likely to form judgements which reflect your own background if you gain a greater understanding of the variety of child rearing patterns and different cultures and religions. For example, some children may not be permitted to eat certain foods. These represent differences to be celebrated.

Confidentiality

Always treat any information about a child or family as confidential. Please see Chapter 6 for a checklist concerning the use of confidential information.

Parental involvement

Parents make valuable contributions to observations as they have an intimate working knowledge of their child in a different setting. Contributions from everyone involved with a child can form the basis of a comprehensive observation.

Involve the child

Contributions from children themselves often bring further insight. By two years of age children are usually more than happy to comment on their own achievements.

Be positive!

Be positive at all times! It is important that you focus on what children can do, not what they cannot do!

Concentrate on children's strengths – not their weaknesses. You can make positive use of children's errors by using them as starting points for their learning. Too frequently assessment has been made to indicate failure and the child has started off at a disadvantage.

FIGURE 1.1   *Parental involvement*

A plea for quality

To achieve a good quality observation and assessment it is essential that you adopt an holistic approach. This means being concerned with the 'whole' child (his/her feelings, attitudes, health, development) and the process by which a child learns and develops through the complex interaction of physical, intellectual, linguistic, social and emotional growth.

Observations and assessments can provide a springboard for reviewing the effectiveness of provision and challenge curriculum developments; they can help us assess health and growth and provide for the needs of the whole child. In the absence of skilled observation and assessment we run the risk of denying children their right to appropriate provision and support.

Observation writing is to be viewed and valued as a lifelong skill. No new invention or piece of equipment will ever be able to replace the use of your own senses.

■ OBSERVING ON A DAILY BASIS

Early years workers spend much of their time looking at and listening to children for many reasons. Carers observe children in order to:

- understand what they are saying
- interpret their demands
- ensure their safety
- monitor their health or illness
- enjoy their company
- join in their play
- ensure fair play
- discover ways which might extend their play
- understand more about the way children learn
- discover the usefulness of any piece of equipment
- appreciate the way children solve problems, initiate friendships and make sense of the world.

Let's consider exactly how adults observe children on a daily basis. They:

- look and follow children's activities
- listen to what they are saying
- tape record their talk, alone, together with other children and with other adults
- video children on their own, with others and with adults
- take photographs
- keep their drawings, paintings and constructions as a reminder of their abilities
- keep school reports and profiles as a reminder of their achievements.

A step on from this 'natural' kind of observing is to plan in advance and record systematically, noting down precise details objectively. This means only recording what you have seen and heard, not what you think happened.

We are the learners!

In many ways observation writing places us, the adults, in a learning position. It is an unjustified and pointless exercise if we are not learning from the information gained. We need to allow observations to modify our opinions. This aim places upon us a requirement to be objective which means keeping to the facts and avoiding untested opinions. The real challenge comes when we take the time to watch and write down what is actually happening.

CHAPTER ONE *Activity*

Objectivity test

Aim: To help you make objective records of observations

From the following statements, choose the most objective:

1 a) M is crying, his face is screwed up and he is rubbing his eyes.

   b) M is unhappy and tired.

2 a) Z is in a temper and hates everybody.

   b) Z is thumping her fist on the back of a chair. She is screwing up her eyes and turning her back on another child.

3 a) R is a clever child. She is good at computers and is looking pleased with herself.

   b) R is looking at the computer, now presses the right key, looks up to check and smiles.

CHAPTER ONE *Activity*

Thinking about feelings

Aim: To help you consider how it might feel to be observed

Children can be quite aware that you are watching them and that you may have a reason for watching them. They may change their behaviour accordingly. So, it is a good idea to know what it feels like to be observed before you try it out on children! Then you will be in a better position to help children feel at ease whilst you observe them.

Ask a partner to observe you whilst you carry out an everyday activity. Perhaps you could be:

■ writing

■ on the telephone

■ comforting your child

■ sharing a story with children

■ talking with parents   ■ planning your work

■ talking with friends   ■ watching the television.

Now think about how it felt to be observed. Did you feel:

uncomfortable? or	comfortable?
aware of observer? or	unaware of observer?
threatened? or	secure?
clumsy? or	relaxed?
self-conscious? or	confident?

After the observation

Now, turn your thoughts to working with children. Discuss any practical ways in which children might be made to feel more at ease whilst being observed.

If you found the process of being observed uncomfortable when observing perhaps you could:

- be discreet, try not to catch the child's eye
- smile if eye contact is made.

If you felt you needed feedback perhaps you could:

- give the child immediate feedback if he/she appears to need it
- be positive in your response.

Summary

- Try to remember the basic concepts.
- An Equal Opportunities Policy must be in operation throughout the whole process.
- Remember that the child may be able to contribute.
- Confidentiality must be maintained during the observation and assessment process.
- Remember that parents and carers know a great deal about their children and can contribute to your work.
- Observation can be included as evidence in an NVQ portfolio.
- Aim to produce an outcome which is positive.

- Adopt an holistic approach to achieve a good quality observation.
- Adults naturally watch children for a variety of reasons and a step on from this 'natural' kind of observing is to plan observations.
- Remind yourself that *you* are the learner.
- Be objective in your observations and assessments.
- Ensure that children feel comfortable while being observed.
- Use the chart to help you monitor your progress.

■ THINKING ABOUT OBSERVING

Portfolio building
- what to include?
- how to use your portfolio

Issues to think through

Why observe?
- developing quality practice

Pass it on?
- whom to pass it on to?
- what to pass on?
- when to pass it on?

What to observe?
- the importance of quality observation
- meeting the requirements of the course
- recognising a suitable opportunity to observe

Making assessments
- background information
- aims
- areas of development
- recommendations
- personal learning
- bibliography

Where to observe?
- working in a variety of settings

Methods of recording observations
- choosing a suitable method
- advantages and disadvantages of each method
- record keeping

How to observe?
- planning
- preparation
- aims
- front sheet
- observing
- evaluations
- presenting work
- getting work assessed

2

Why Observe?

Aims

The aims of this chapter are to look at observing from the points of view of:

■ the observer

■ the child and parents

■ other professionals.

Watching children is not new or difficult. Parents and early years workers find children original and fascinating and gain a great deal of pleasure from listening to and watching them. The more you listen and watch the more you will want to know!

Channelling this curiosity and fascination for the benefit of the child is the challenge for parents, observers and other professionals.

■ WHY BE AN OBSERVER?

Observation, recording and assessment are all invaluable professional tools worth developing and perfecting. Observations should become an intrinsic part of the practice of all early years workers.

As an observer you can learn about children and build up a body of knowledge which enables you to play a unique part in their lives. You will begin to understand the wide range of normal growth and development as you link theory with practice. By looking in depth at what you are observing you will be able to analyse your findings. This in turn will influence your practice. Observing can be a tool to find out how your skills are developing, not just how the child is progressing. For example, if you have made a change in something you were doing you could use observations and assessments to find out how successful this has been.

Observing becomes a dynamic process if it is used in a pro-active way. This should be the objective of all early years workers. An example of this approach is evident in the High Scope curriculum. See Chapter 6, pages 62–64 for further information on High Scope.

■ WHY ARE OBSERVATIONS IMPORTANT TO CHILDREN AND PARENTS?

Children and parents are entitled to expect the highest quality in child care practice. Observing is an essential element in achieving quality child care practice because it helps you to 'know' a child. It leads to an understanding of a child's developmental needs and on to appropriate planning, building on a child's developmental strengths.

Early years workers are partners with parents as together they learn and become experts about the child. In a good partnership parents will feel safe to register any concerns they may have about their child's development or behaviour with the early years workers. Your observations may provide the key to identifying a difficulty a child may be experiencing, perhaps a slight hearing or visual difficulty, or the need to adjust to the arrival of a new baby in the family.

The more you understand about children the more your confidence as an observer will grow. You will become more interested in the strategies and processes through which children work and in how they use their environment.

■ WHY DO OTHER PROFESSIONALS OBSERVE CHILDREN?

Professionals observe young children for a range of planning, monitoring and research reasons.

Educational setting

The key reasons for observing young children in an educational setting are to find out their existing expertise and to use observations to feed an assessment of why children exhibit such behaviours. Early years workers can then ensure that access to learning (planned in the curriculum) is available to all children. Accurate observation can facilitate curriculum planning within the classroom. It can assist with structured profiles, monitoring and referral and the writing of an Individual Education Plan (IEP).

Health surveillance

Observation based on sound knowledge of child development plays a key role as part of child health surveillance and is of particular importance now that the number of routine developmental examinations are reduced. Resources are now targeted where help and care is thought to be needed most.

Professionals may be alerted by parents or early years workers to mild or more serious concerns about a child's development or behaviour. Objective observational skills are an important part of the process of accurate assessment concerning the child's needs and give vital clues as to how child care workers and other professionals should respond. Many records, particularly health records, are held by parents. (See Chapter 6, pages 73–75.)

Early years workers and other professionals must regard the information they hold about a child as confidential. You need to be clear that you are working as part of a multidisciplinary team and need to know how and when to pass on information gained from observing. You can read more about this in Chapter 8.

Individual programmes for children or care plans (for example relating to a medical difficulty) must be based on sound observational knowledge of the child, as should contributions to case conferences, health surveillance or court proceedings.

FIGURES 2.1A, B *Making observations and assessments is a basis for good practice*

■ PLANNING CHILDREN'S ACTIVITIES

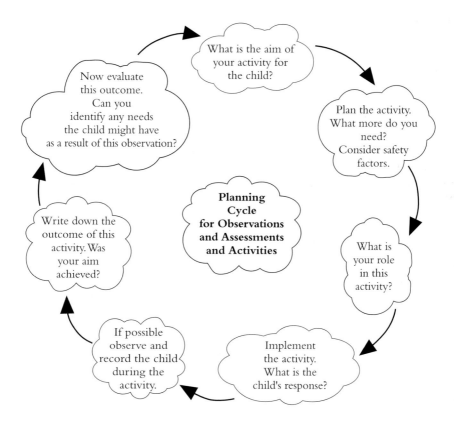

What is the aim of your activity for the child?

Plan the activity. What more do you need? Consider safety factors.

Now evaluate this outcome. Can you identify any needs the child might have as a result of this observation?

Planning Cycle for Observations and Assessments and Activities

What is your role in this activity?

Write down the outcome of this activity. Was your aim achieved?

If possible observe and record the child during the activity.

Implement the activity. What is the child's response?

Planning for activities requires clear objectives. What do you hope the child will learn? What should be the outcome? Observations followed by assessments help you to know which activities would be most beneficial to a child at any given time. It will help you meet the child at their point of growth and enable you to provide resources which are stimulating and appropriate.

FIGURE 2.2 *Developing fine motor skills*

CHAPTER TWO *Activity*

Thinking about suitable activities

Aim: To help you consider suitable activities to further develop fine motor skills

The child in Figure 2.2 is obviously enjoying this activity and is developing fine motor skills.

■ Can you think of other activities which encourage this area of development?

■ How would you plan for these activities?

■ What resources would you need for these activities?

■ Consider your role whilst carrying out your chosen activities.

Try to make an opportunity to stand back in your workplace for ten minutes and keep the following question in mind.

'Is there anything in the layout of the environment which could be improved to allow the children greater access to equipment?'

Quality control

- Professional workers with children believe that all children have a right to be observed and an individual learning programme devised.
- As a professional worker the safety and well-being of young children must always be your prime concern. Observing young children will sharpen your awareness of potential hazards and issues to do with health and safety.
- You can update your information by research into books on child development, journals, articles and computer networks. These will help to deepen your understanding of child development.

In-depth discussion

Standing back for short periods during your work will give you a clearer picture of your own role. You will be able to see how other adults and professionals meet the needs of young children and you can, if appropriate, adopt their ideas and strategies. If you are more experienced at observing young children you will find that a fresh look at why you observe will increase your motivation and perhaps bring about a revision in your practice.

Summary

- Observing children presents us with a fascinating challenge.
- Children and parents are entitled to quality child care practice.
- It is important to develop a good partnership with parents.
- Professionals use observations for the purposes of planning, monitoring and researching.
- Observations and assessments will help you to identify appropriate activities.
- It is important to continually review your own practice.

■ THINKING ABOUT OBSERVING

Portfolio building
- what to include?
- how to use your portfolio

Issues to think through

Why observe?
- developing quality practice

Pass it on?
- whom to pass it on to?
- what to pass on?
- when to pass it on?

What to observe?
- the importance of quality observation
- meeting the requirements of the course
- recognising a suitable opportunity to observe

Making assessments
- background information
- aims
- areas of development
- recommendations
- personal learning
- bibliography

Where to observe?
- working in a variety of settings

Methods of recording observations
- choosing a suitable method
- advantages and disadvantages of each method
- record keeping

How to observe?
- planning
- preparation
- aims
- front sheet
- observing
- evaluations
- presenting work
- getting work assessed

What to Observe?

■ WHAT SHOULD THE CHILDREN BE DOING?

You can observe children doing just about anything!
exploring • making discoveries • when ill • talking •
puzzling over problems • being mobile • watching TV •
agonising over choices • making friends • inventing •
crying • being alone • playing alone • convalescing
after illness • interacting with adults • making jokes •
being comforted • comforting an injured friend •
having tantrums • drawing

There is a great deal to learn about children. The possibilities are endless! Watching children regularly will help you understand how they interact with each other and with their environment, and about how you can meet their needs.

FIGURE 3.1A, B, C, D *You can observe children doing just about anything*

■ DIFFERENT COURSE REQUIREMENTS

If you are building a portfolio for either a course or NVQ assessment you will need to demonstrate the ability to observe accurately and skilfully.

Observation for NVQ assessment will need to be discussed with your assessor. Child observations can be included in most units for the Early Years Care and Education NVQ and can be presented in a portfolio. NVQ Mandatory Unit C.16 'Observe and Assess the Development and Behaviour of Children' occurs in all Level 3 qualifications. Students on an early years course will be advised by a tutor which observations are to be done, how many and the range to be covered. The method used for these observations may vary. Read Chapter 6 in order to decide the most appropriate way to go about each observation.

Other courses such as the CACHE Diploma in Child Care and Education, the NCA Level 3 Certificate in Childminding Practice or the Edexcel (BTEC) National Certificate in Early Years Level 3 will have particular specifications.

A range of aspects to observe

It is important to understand that there is a range of aspects to observe. Any file or portfolio of observation will need to demonstrate a breadth of understanding concerning child development and behaviour.

It might be useful to think of the term 'range' as including each of the following.

1 Development (e.g. physical development or language development)
2 Settings (e.g. home or nursery school)
3 Behaviour (e.g. distressed or independent)
4 Age (e.g. two years or five-and-a-half years)
5 Social setting (e.g. alone or in large groups)
6 Play and learning (e.g. parallel play or early numeracy)
7 Health (e.g. hygiene routines or hearing test)
8 Methods (e.g. checklist or free description)

The chart on page 16 gives more detail of these eight areas and can be used for reference. You can identify each completed observation with a tick or by using colour coding. Be guided by your tutor.

Quality control

Don't forget to maintain confidentiality! Once you have decided whom to observe do remember to gain permission first. You should avoid using the child's real name and any other means of identifying the child, family or staff.

Ensuring a range of observations

7–8 years	6–7 years	4–5 years	3–4 years	2–3 years	18 mths – 2yrs	1 yr – 18 mths	9 mths–1 year	6–9 months	4–6 months	2–4 months	0–2 months	
												Physical development
												Intellectual development
												Language development
												Emotional development
												Moral development
												Physical care and routines
												Early learning
												Focus on particular needs
												Hearing test
												Home setting in/outdoors
												Hospital setting
												Nursery setting in/outdoors
												Day Care Centre in/outdoors
												Reception class in/outdoors
												Yr. 1/2 in/outdoors
												Other setting
												Distressed behaviour
												Independent behaviour
												Difficult behaviour
												Contented behaviour
												Creative and imaginative play
												Constructive play
												Role play
												Solo play
												Parallel play
												Co-operative play
												Complex co-operative play
												Small groups
												Large groups
												Written account method
												Time sample method
												Event sample method
												Checklist method
												Longitudinal method
												Tape/video
												Other

■ GETTING STARTED

It is probably best to begin by observing a child playing on his/her own. Observing a group of children is more demanding and should be left until you feel more confident. Your tutor or assessor is likely to specify your first observation, perhaps suggesting you observe a child playing with a jigsaw puzzle. Placement supervisors may help you choose a child and advise you about suitable times to observe. Sometimes your placement supervisor will ask you to observe a child for a particular reason. This is a good opportunity to make a useful contribution to your workplace and at the same time contribute to your own portfolio file.

Particular interests

If you have a particular interest or you would like to specialise in a certain area in the future it would be good for your file to demonstrate this interest or expertise, in addition to fulfilling the particular requirements of the course.

FIGURE 3.2A *Playing ball*

Inspiration!

If you are finding it difficult to choose and be inspired, look through the following photographs of children in different settings. Each of these situations could prompt a worthwhile observation.

FIGURE 3.2B *Cooking activity*

FIGURE 3.2C *Imaginative play*

FIGURE 3.2D *Sharing books*

FIGURE 3.2E *Discovery play*

FIGURE 3.2F *Water play*

FIGURE 3.2G *Parallel play*

FIGURE 3.2H *Child with pet*

FIGURE 3.2I *Play with best friend*

FIGURE 3.2J *Gross motor play*

FIGURE 3.2K *Problem solving with a friend*

FIGURE 3.2L *Table-top play*

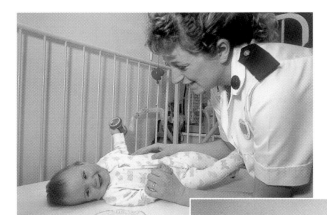

FIGURE 3.2M *Baby in hospital*

FIGURE 3.2N *Child cleaning teeth*

FIGURE 3.2O *Child helping tidy up*

Summary

- Children present us with numerous opportunities to learn about them. Train yourself to recognise those opportunities when they arise.

- Be sure that you understand the observational requirements of the course you are following.

- NVQ candidates can discuss what to observe with their assessor.

- Ensure that you understand the meaning of the word 'range' in the context of observations. Use the chart on page 16 to help you.

- Don't forget to ask permission to observe.

- Start with an observation which involves only one child.

- Look through the photographs on pages 18–23 for inspiration.

■ THINKING ABOUT OBSERVING

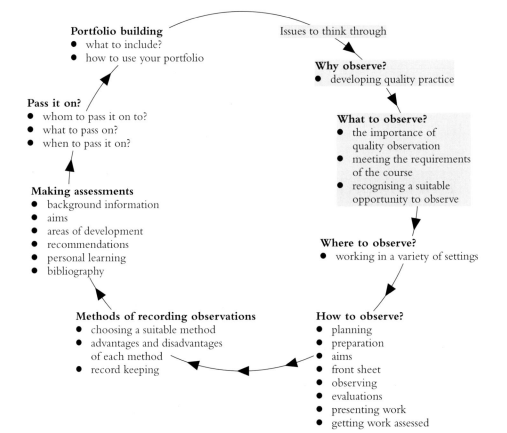

Portfolio building
- what to include?
- how to use your portfolio

Issues to think through

Why observe?
- developing quality practice

Pass it on?
- whom to pass it on to?
- what to pass on?
- when to pass it on?

What to observe?
- the importance of quality observation
- meeting the requirements of the course
- recognising a suitable opportunity to observe

Making assessments
- background information
- aims
- areas of development
- recommendations
- personal learning
- bibliography

Where to observe?
- working in a variety of settings

Methods of recording observations
- choosing a suitable method
- advantages and disadvantages of each method
- record keeping

How to observe?
- planning
- preparation
- aims
- front sheet
- observing
- evaluations
- presenting work
- getting work assessed

4

Where to Observe?

Aims

The aims of this chapter are to:

- identify appropriate places to carry out observations

- identify reasons for observing children in a variety of situations

- give examples of how the NVQ Early Years Option Units help you plan for observations which focus on the work setting

- help you recognise good practice when observing other adults

- help you know how to observe adults sensitively

- help you consider what to do if you disagree with the practice you are observing

- help you ensure continuity between settings

- identify and use a variety of methods of observing in different settings

- help you consider when observation outside the placement may be applicable

- help you consider how the physical environment affects children

- help you consider voluntary work as a means of gaining experience

- help you identify the use of a diary for establishing good practice.

■ A VARIETY OF SETTINGS

Students studying child development on a course are usually offered a variety of settings in which to learn about the day-to-day running of the establishment and become a member of the working team. This enables the student to add to their general knowledge of child development and ensures that the essential criteria of a range of observations is met.

Students are usually offered placements with either day care centres, families, nurseries, schools, hospitals and possibly other settings available in the area. Each course or programme has its own arrangements concerning the length of time spent in each placement. Sometimes the arrangement is one or two days each week, or it can be whole weeks or block periods.

These placements will give you the opportunity to observe and learn about:

- how children interact with other children
- how children behave when they play alone
- how children interact with adults
- how children interact with siblings, parents or carers at home
- how children respond to a structured learning environment
- how children respond to a free play situation
- how children bring and share their own cultural heritage
- how children develop at different rates.

■ NVQ OPTIONS

Candidates undertaking NVQs will (as well as undertaking the Mandatory Units) also do Option Units which will focus on their work setting.

The following are fourteen units suitable for a whole qualification in a Group Setting at Level 3 (three Option Units can be selected, as appropriate, for a Group Setting). Details about the Elements of each unit, the Range, the Performance Criteria, the different methods of assessment, together with the Knowledge Evidence, can be found in the National Occupational Standards for Early Years Care and Education, listed in the Further Reading Chapter.

Mandatory Units

C 2	Provide for children's physical needs
C 3	Promote the physical development of children
C 5	Promote children's social and emotional development
C 7	Provide a framework for the management of children's behaviour
C 10	Promote children's sensory and intellectual development
C 11	Promote children's language and communication development
C 15	Contribute to the protection of children from abuse
C 16	Observe and assess the development and behaviour of children
E 3	Plan and equip environments for children
M 7	Plan, implement and evaluate learning activities and experiences
P 2	Establish and maintain relationships with parents

Option Units

(Three to be selected from these four examples to complete the fourteen needed for the Level 3 Qualification)

See National Occupational Standards for further Option Units.

C 14	Care for and promote the development of babies
C 24	Work with other professionals
M 7	Support the development of children's Literacy Skills
M 8	Plan implement and evaluate routines for young children

Unit C16 (listed in the Mandatory Units above) occurs in all Level 3 Qualifications. (From *The National Occupational Standards for Early Years Care and Education*)

■ OBSERVING OTHER ADULTS

Whilst you are observing children in early years settings you will, of course, be aware of how other early years workers actually work with young children. This is a good opportunity for you to add to your knowledge of how to cope in various situations. You will learn how experienced early years workers help children in difficult situations. In this way you add to your repertoire of caring for young children.

If a student is having difficulty managing a group of children, good placement supervisors will recommend that the student takes a few minutes during the day just to observe how other early years workers provide for the children. Students find this enormously helpful because they are able to stand back, observe and then analyse exactly what is going on and why it works.

In-depth discussion

If you already hold a position as an early years worker why not ask someone to video you at work? However pleasing or painful this may be it can be helpful to identify ways of improving your practice.

■ WHAT IF I DISAGREE WITH THE PRACTICE I SEE?

Generally you will observe good practice in each setting. It is important not to become disheartened if the practice you see sometimes does not match up to what you have read and been taught.

If it is necessary for you to include and record in an observation what another adult is saying or doing, try to be sensitive in the way you record this. Remember most child care workers try very hard to provide a good service for young children. Occasionally they have off days – just as everyone does! If you have serious concerns about a child care worker's practice talk to your tutor or assessor.

■ ESTABLISHING CONTINUITY BETWEEN SETTINGS

It would be ideal to observe the same child or group of children in a variety of settings over a period of time. Through this a truly comprehensive picture of this child or group can be gained. Unfortunately, this is rarely possible. However, using a variety of methods of observing will add to the validity of your work. You will provide a more realistic picture of the child's development or behaviour because you examine it in a number of different ways. Establishing continuity between one type of provision and another can be achieved in some ways by passing on information gained from observations and assessments.

It is inevitable that there are interruptions in a child's life such as illness, moving house, separation or divorce of parents. In some cases the early years worker may be the only constant factor in the child's life. You can help to ensure that each child's experience is stable and secure whilst he or she is in your care. Observations and assessments can help to establish connections between each day of a child's experience in the care and education environment. These connections can also be made between settings. Good record keeping born out of accurate observations can be passed on to the next setting. This can ensure that provision for each child builds on past experience. When to pass on information is dealt with more fully in Chapter 8.

■ OBSERVATIONS OUTSIDE PLACEMENTS

Students often ask tutors if they can make observations outside their placement. For example, you babysit for a neighbour, and a situation has arisen with the child which would benefit your studies – observing the child communicating with a younger sibling, for instance. Each course has its own policy about this. You will need to gain permission and a signature from the adult responsible for the child.

■ THE PHYSICAL ENVIRONMENT

Sometimes observations can require you to look closely at the care and education environment. You may be asked to carry out an observation like this one:

'Observe, on one occasion, a group of children in one area of the care and education environment. Note how this physical environment affects the children's play.'

In this type of observation you are required to look at the way the physical environment contributes to the children's play. Again, experience in a variety of settings will help you analyse in an informed manner.

CHAPTER FOUR *Activity*

Considering the layout of the environment

Aim: To help you think about planning for play once an observation has taken place

Let's assume that you have just observed a group of five four-year-olds involved in a junk modelling activity. You have observed that the layout of the room discourages the smooth running of their play. Plan out and draw a satisfactory layout of a room, which allows for independence in their play. The children need to have access to drawers or containers for this activity.

■ VOLUNTARY WORK

It is very important to obtain as much experience of working in a variety of places as possible. Working during the holidays – perhaps in a voluntary capacity – will give you a broad foundation of experience which will help you when applying for jobs. For example, you may be the only applicant for a job who has had experience of working with profoundly deaf children and the employer just happens to need someone with this particular experience! If you offer your services as a volunteer early years worker you may find that only a few weeks' work of a particular nature may extend you in a way that is really valuable or relevant later on.

■ KEEPING A DIARY

Keeping a diary of each day in your placement will help you in many ways.

- It will provide your assessor or tutor with a picture of what you are able to provide for young children in terms of planning and preparation.
- It should provide a useful store of ideas of suitable activities for the future.
- It should be useful as evidence for a portfolio for NVQ assessment.
- It can help you chart your own progression and development and identify your strengths and weaknesses.

Summary

- Make good use of every opportunity to observe children.
- Try to gain experience of working in a variety of settings.
- Establish continuity between placements for the child.
- Use a variety of methods of observing in each placement.
- Consider voluntary work as a means of extending your knowledge.
- Keep a diary.

■ THINKING ABOUT OBSERVING

Portfolio building
- what to include?
- how to use your portfolio

Issues to think through

Why observe?
- developing quality practice

Pass it on?
- whom to pass it on to?
- what to pass on?
- when to pass it on?

What to observe?
- the importance of quality observation
- meeting the requirements of the course
- recognising a suitable opportunity to observe

Making assessments
- background information
- aims
- areas of development
- recommendations
- personal learning
- bibliography

Where to observe?
- working in a variety of settings

Methods of recording observations
- choosing a suitable method
- advantages and disadvantages of each method
- record keeping

How to observe?
- planning
- preparation
- aims
- front sheet
- observing
- evaluations
- presenting work
- getting work assessed

5

How to Observe?

Aims

The aim of this chapter is to guide you through each step of the observation:

- planning
- preparation
- writing an aim
- completing the front sheet and making a start at observing
- choosing the best place to sit when observing.

In this chapter we will consider how to:

- deal with your concerns about observing
- observe a group of children
- build your confidence as an observer
- present your work
- get your work assessed once you have evaluated the observation
- ensure confidentiality and objectivity.

■ A STEP-BY-STEP GUIDE TO YOUR FIRST OBSERVATION

You can now consider how to go about your first observation. Some courses on child development will tell you exactly which observations are required and most will tell you exactly how many you need to do. NVQ candidates will be helped by their assessor to plan.

Your tutor will talk you through your first observation so that you understand the objectives. Let's assume that you have been given the following observation.

'Observe, on one occasion, a child playing alone.' This observation should last about ten minutes.

Step 1. Planning

This observation is a fairly straightforward one with which to start. The first step is to think about what you need to do before you start. You need to consider the following:

- Which child should you observe? (Your placement supervisor will advise you.)
- Seek permission to observe this child.
- Is the observation relevant to the place where you are working? In other words, is it possible?
- Once you have gained permission it is courteous to tell other adults present what you are doing.
- Decide on a time which is convenient for you to undertake your observation.
- Which method of observing will you use? (See Chapter 6 for choice of methods.)
- Which resources will you need?

Step 2. Preparation

This checklist should help you.

- pen
- pencil
- rubber
- notebook
- camera
- video
- tape-recorder and tape
- watch
- pre-coded forms

Let's assume that this observation is going to be carried out using the free description method which is explained in Chapter 6.

When you have planned and prepared you are nearly ready to begin. But let's just stop here and look at the very important subject of aims.

Step 3. Aims

Unless you are observing on the spur of the moment you will have specific aims in mind.

Getting the aim of the observation right takes a little while so it is worth spending time practising. Later on you will find that writing up your evaluation will depend on what you have written for your aim.

Your aims might concern the observation of:

- a child demonstrating a particular skill or behaviour
- a child interacting with others
- a sick child
- a child during convalescence and rehabilitation.

FIGURE 5.1   *Discovering music*

CHAPTER FIVE *Activity*

Thinking about aims

Aim: To identify reasons for observing and to learn how to write a sensible aim

Think of a child in your workplace and concentrate on one particular skill that you have noticed this child developing, for example cutting with scissors.
   Now complete this phrase.

'I aim to observe X's ....

and to note down' ....

For example: 'I aim to observe X's fine motor skills and to note down his/her enjoyment of the activity.'
   Try this exercise again, thinking about another child.
   Talk this over with a partner and consider whether the aims you have chosen are realistic.

Quality control

You may not have time to consider an aim. The observation may be spontaneous. This can be just as valid. Although it is best to consider your aim first, remember to be observant at all times.

CHAPTER FIVE *Activity*

Thinking more about aims

Aim: To help you be specific when writing aims for observations and assessments

FIGURE 5.2   *Hand washing provides an opportunity to experiment*

As you know water has fascinating properties. Whilst adults may have hygiene in mind children see washing hands as an opportunity to experiment! Think of two aims for observing a child washing his/her hands.

Writing aims in a straightforward manner helps you to focus on particular skills or behaviour and should prevent you attempting the impossible. Consider the following aim.

'Observe X playing alone in the sandpit and note his physical, emotional, social and intellectual development' . . . and all in 10 minutes!'

This sort of aim is far too ambitious. No one could possibly achieve all this is one observation. So keep your aim within your grasp, then when you come to write up the evaluation you will find that you have focused on specific areas, and you will be able to make sense of what you have seen.

Step 4. Completing a front sheet

You may photocopy the front sheet on page 39. This is an example of a standard pro forma. You should always complete a front sheet – this will help you get into the habit of gathering all the essential information.

- Note down the time you are starting.
- Ask yourself if you know of any factors which might have a bearing on the child's behaviour at the time, e.g. if the child has a cold. Note these down.
- Note the number of children and other adults present at the time.

Step 5. Observing

Note down anything the child says. Make your notes in the present tense, for example 'X is standing on her left foot'. Note down whether the child uses the right or left hand – or both. What does the child's face look like? For example, note down if the child's tongue is hanging out, or his/her eyes are screwing up? What sort of grip is the child using? Is it a palmar grasp? Note down any other aspect of this child's play that seems important. Stop after ten minutes of observing.

If something interesting is going on or if you do not yet have enough information, continue, stating that you have done this.

Now make a note of the time the observation ended. You have now completed the necessary information for the main body of the observation.

This kind of focused observation should not be inconvenient to the workplace and will enable you to quickly get back into the routine of working with the children.

Quality control

It has been known for placement supervisors to complain that a whole morning has been taken up by a student doing one observation! This has prevented the student interacting with the children. Obviously this kind of time commitment is unnecessary. Observational work must be balanced against the needs of the child being observed and the placement. When you are observing remember to be objective. This means: *keep to the facts.* Note down what is actually happening – not your interpretation or what you would like to happen.

New observers often worry about what is expected of them in certain situations. You may be asking yourself 'what should I do if the child hurts herself?' while the observation is taking place. Of course, you must stop the observation immediately and comfort the child if there are no other adults nearby to help. Your prime concern must always be the safety and well-being of the child.

Where to sit

You might be wondering where it is best to stand or sit when observing children. The answer really depends on your aims and which method of observing you have chosen. Sitting a short distance away from the children and being as unobtrusive as possible is important. This means not creating a great flurry and disturbance or drawing attention to yourself in any way. It should then be possible for you to swiftly note down what the children are doing, but you will not be able to carry on a conversation yourself with the children, or perhaps catch everything they say. Children may find this style of observing hard to accept unless you are very unobtrusive.

Figure 5.3 *'Unobstrusive observer'*

Participant observer

Sitting close to the children will enable you to carry on a conversation with them, but this will stop you from noting down everything they are doing.

In a bid for full attention a child once said to an observer 'You are not listening to me. Put the pencil down and talk to me.' Needless to say, that is exactly what the observer did!

However, a different response from another observer was also successful. She smiled and said to the child that she really wanted to remember all the good things that were happening so she needed to write them down. The child agreed, understood and was interested in seeing the notes at the end of the session. A valuable opportunity was gained for the child to observe the adult writing for a purpose. He later was seen to sit with a clipboard, paper and pencil beside his friend.

You may be wondering also what happens if while you are engaged in observing solo play in the sandpit, another child grabs the spade and a fight ensues. You should leave the observation and help calm the situation down. If your aim is to observe a child playing alone and another child joins in the play, it is best to carry on observing as you might find the interaction interesting. Many students worry that they won't be able to write everything down. This is a good reason for looking carefully at your aims. It could be that you are attempting too much or you may need to develop your own form of shorthand.

Observing a group of children

Observing more than one child usually means that you will need to share out your attention between the children. It does not mean that you have to write more but you will have to be very focused in your watching and listening. Think carefully

FIGURES 5.4A, B
'Participant observer'

about your aims and concentrate *only* on those particular aims. For example it could be that your aims were to observe the interaction between the children and to note their use of language.

Step 6. Evaluating

This is covered in Chapter 7, Making Assessments.

Building confidence

If your first observation turns out to be a disaster don't worry about it! The first few are often very difficult. Just have another go and you will find your ability to record what is happening will improve with each attempt.

Figure 5.5 *Small group play*

Step 7. Presentation of your work

If you are an NVQ candidate you should add your observations to your portfolio and discuss them with your assessor. Putting your work in a plastic folder will help to keep it in good condition. Your notes during the observation now need to be written up neatly. You can use a word processor or handwriting providing it is legible! Presentation is important although it is the content of your work that really matters.

Step 8. Getting your work assessed

Once you have written the assessment, made recommendations, written your personal learning and written a bibliography, you are ready to hand in your work to your supervisor, assessor or tutor. (Turn to Chapter 7 for advice on making assessments.)

It is best to hand your work in regularly so that you obtain the necessary feedback. Handing in twenty observations on the same day will make things difficult for the person marking them and you may become despondent when you realise that you have made the same error in each piece of work.

No assessor or tutor will expect you to get everything right at the first attempt. However, all assessors and tutors are looking for willingness to learn. It is progress indeed to hear a student say 'Well, I didn't know that about X. In future I will be able to help her to . . .'

At this point you might like to turn to pages 41 and 42 to read an example of a real observation.

Confidentiality and objectivity

Parents and carers have a right to see anything you write about their child and they may wish to contribute their own comments. Again, do check that you are allowed to use the information. At times you may be given further information which helps you understand a child's behaviour better.

Remember to ask if you can include the information: confidentiality at all times is very important.

Most students find it quite a sobering thought to imagine a parent or carer looking over their shoulder reading observations of the child. It is important to take great care to be objective in your comments.

■ OBSERVATIONS WHICH MAY FORM EVIDENCE FOR SUSPECTED CHILD ABUSE

You will need to make sure that your observation of the child's behaviour, appearance and physical condition or health are not obtrusive.

You will need to record any significant changes in the child's behaviour, appearance and physical condition or health.

Your recording must be factual and accurate. You must not include your impressions, but remain objective. Chapter 8 discusses making assessments and when to pass on information.

CHAPTER FIVE *Activity*

Maintaining objectivity in observing

Aim: To ensure objectivity in your observation

When it is convenient, ask another child care worker to observe a certain child at the same time as you. Then compare notes, looking carefully at the way you have both described what the child is doing.

■ COMPLETING THE FRONT SHEET

It helps to have a standard form which you always use so that you get into the habit of gathering all the necessary information. These notes will help you fill in the standard front sheet on page 39, which you can photocopy.

Observation and assessment number. This is the order in which you have done the observation and assessments, regardless of the type of observation. The moderator will want to see your file and will be looking to see how you have progressed. The number can be referenced in your portfolio.

NVQ Link. Discuss with your assessor and refer to *The National Occupational Standards for Early Years Care and Education*.

Date observation took place. The date the observation took place should be recorded – not the date you write it up.

This page may be photocopied for your own use.

Observations AND ASSESSMENTS FRONT SHEET

Observer's name
....

Observation and/or assessment number/portfolio reference
....

NVQ link
....

Date observation took place
....

Time observation started
....

Time observation ended
....

This observation took place at
....

Number of children and adults present during observation
....

Child/children's identity to be known as
....

Age of child/children in years and months
....

Gender
....

Permission granted (signature)
....

Tutor's signature
....

The aim(s) and purpose(s) of this observation
....

The method used for this observation
....

The setting for this observation
....

Time observation started. Record the time you picked up your pencil and notebook.

Time observation ended. Record the time you put down your pencil and notebook.

The observation took place at. The type of setting should be entered here, e.g. nursery class. Do not write, for example, the name of the school.

Number of children and adults present during observation. Look around and count up. You might need this information when you make an assessment.

Child/children's identity to be known as. Use X, Y or Z or change the child's first name completely. (Many children have names which could be easily identified.) Similarly you should never name a member of staff or a parent or carer. You could write 'the early years worker' or 'parent' or 'carer'.

Age of child/children in years and months. For example, 'five years and three months'. This needs to be correct in order that you make an accurate assessment. A few months can make a great difference.

Gender. For some observations this information will be important; therefore it is a good idea to get into the habit of recording it.

Permission granted (signature). Your placement supervisor is usually the person to sign. This proves that the observation really took place. If you wish to include photographs, children's drawings or their work you must remember to seek permission.

Tutor's signature. Your tutor will probably want to sign this once the work is ready to be marked.

The aim(s) or purpose(s) of this observation. Start like this: 'To observe X's . . . skills/behaviour and to note . . .' (See pages 31 to 33 for further guidance.)

The method used for this observation. See Chapter 6 for the range of methods.

The setting for this observation. See Chapter 4 for settings. Don't write the name of the placement. Under this heading you should record any background information which would help the reader make sense of the context. For example, you might like to specify exactly the location within the class, for example 'at the computer'.

■ A COMPLETED OBSERVATION

The following observation is an original one carried out by an NNEB student. The front sheet and main body of the observation are shown but the evaluation is not shown because this will be looked at in Chapter 7. This observation is regarded as a satisfactory example of this type of recording.

Observations AND ASSESSMENTS FRONT SHEET

Observations and Assessments Front Sheet

Observer's name   R. Hyde

Observation and/or assessment number/portfolio reference   13

NVQ link

Date observation took place	20.4.94
Time observation started	14.30
Time observation ended	14.38
This observation took place at	A primary school
Number of children and adults present during observation	30 children 2 adults
Child/children's identity to be known as	T
Age of child/children in years and months	6 years 2 months
Gender	Female
Permission granted (signature)	A. N. Other
Tutor's signature	J. Smith

The aim(s) and purpose(s) of this observation   To observe T whilst she plays on the school computer and to note her hand eye co-ordination, concentration and interest in the programme.

The method used for this observation   free description

The setting for this observation   T has just come in from play and is sitting near the window.

The setting of this observation: In a classroom. T is playing on the computer. Thirty pupils are involved with other activities in the room.

T sits on the stool in front of the computer left foot tapping. T looks at the computer. T's eyes move from side to side. She moves the top half of her body forwards and backwards, whilst sitting on her stool. T's hands are lying flat on top of the keyboard. She looks down at it. T moves her right hand to right side of the keyboard and presses a key using her index finger. T's left hand is kept still. T now looks up at the screen whilst pressing the key. 'Oh, no'. Eyes creased up. T's right hand releases and gets placed flat under her chin. The right elbow is supported by the computer table. T looks down at the keyboard. T looks up at the screen and her eyes move from side to side. Then T looks down at the keyboard. T now releases her right hand and moves both hands down the keyboard to the space bar. T uses the tips of her fingers of each hand to press down the bar. She looks up at the screen. Both hands move down and sit on her lap. T's eyes move from side to side. T moves the top half of her body backwards and forwards whilst sitting on the stool. T looks down at the keyboard and bends her head slightly to the left. T now brings both hands from her lap to the keyboard. The left hand lays flat on top of the board. The right hand moves to the left side of the keyboard and presses a key using her index finger. She smiles and pokes her tongue out. T raises her head and looks up at the screen. She lifts her right hand and points to the screen with her index finger. 'All their food has been eaten.' (T reads aloud from the screen). She looks down at the keyboard. Both hands press down on the space bar. T looks at the screen. T's eyes move from side to side. 'Shall I pick 1 or 2? Um?' (T reads aloud from the screen). T looks down at the keyboard. T's right hand moves to the left across the keyboard and presses a key using her index finger. She looks at the screen. Eyes moving left to right. 'Now find the other half.' (T reads aloud from the screen). T looks down at the keyboard and her left hand moves across the left side of the keyboard and presses a key using her index finger. 'Ah, I did it!' T smiles, showing her teeth. T moves backwards and forwards on her chair. Both hands are clenched on either side of her stool. She is still. T looks at the screen. (The teacher tells the class to pack away). T stands up from her stool and walks away.

Summary

- Step 1. Plan carefully.
- Step 2. Prepare and assemble your equipment.
- Step 3. Think about your aims.
- Step 4. Complete your front sheet.

- Step 5. Observe.
- Step 6. Make an assessment.
- Step 7. Present your work.
- Step 8. Hand in your work for marking.

■ THINKING ABOUT OBSERVING

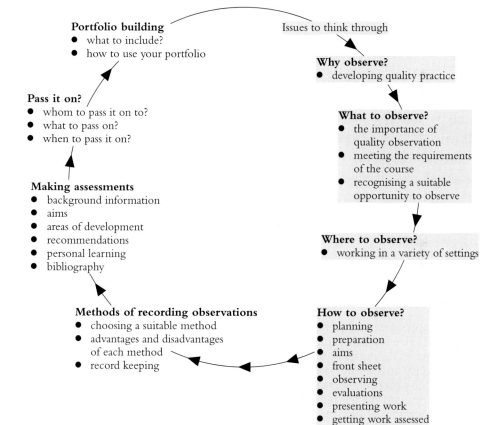

Portfolio building
- what to include?
- how to use your portfolio

Issues to think through

Why observe?
- developing quality practice

Pass it on?
- whom to pass it on to?
- what to pass on?
- when to pass it on?

What to observe?
- the importance of quality observation
- meeting the requirements of the course
- recognising a suitable opportunity to observe

Making assessments
- background information
- aims
- areas of development
- recommendations
- personal learning
- bibliography

Where to observe?
- working in a variety of settings

Methods of recording observations
- choosing a suitable method
- advantages and disadvantages of each method
- record keeping

How to observe?
- planning
- preparation
- aims
- front sheet
- observing
- evaluations
- presenting work
- getting work assessed

6

Methods of Recording Observations

Aims

The aims of this chapter are to:

■ describe a number of methods for observing

■ help you gain an understanding of a variety of methods

■ help you identify the best method for each of your observations

■ encourage you to test out methods and to rate their effectiveness

■ provide you with examples of existing methods of record keeping.

It is important to choose the appropriate method of recording if you are to achieve accurate results.

In this chapter a variety of methods are described and examples given. It is suggested that you try them out and judge their effectiveness for yourself. Any method of recording needs to be 'backed up' by the use of other methods. This will ensure reliability and validity in your work.

Beware of any method which indicates a bias in terms of stereotyping. Remember that all children will demonstrate their true capabilities in an environment which reflects their individual identity.

Here are some questions for you to consider:

■ Does the method encourage parental contribution?
■ Does the method allow the child to contribute?
■ Is the format of the method suitable for all children, whatever their special learning needs or abilities?
■ Is the method sensitive to the cultural heritage and variety of languages of the children and their families?
■ Is the method appropriate for the working environment?

Helpful hint

There is a wide variety of terms used to describe each method of recording. The description of the method is more important than its title! You must take time to ensure that you understand exactly what each method can achieve for you.

■ SOME TECHNIQUES OF OBSERVING

More detailed descriptions of the following methods can be found on pages 46–51.

Time sampling

Time sampling is a particular method of observing a child or children at fixed intervals over a period of time. For example, you may be concerned about a child's ability to establish relationships with other children or adults. By observing and recording on a regular basis, an accurate picture of what the child is doing and with whom the child is making contact can be established.

Another reason for observing may be to find out how frequently a piece of equipment is being used. This method of time sampling would be appropriate in this case.

Time sampling may be used when there needs to be a focus on a child's behaviour. There may also be concerns about a child's behaviour, for example if the child is:

- shy and withdrawn
- frequently thumb-sucking
- frequently crying
- frequently masturbating
- constantly tired.

It is normally considered that two minutes for a time sample is ideal. However, smaller or larger units of time might be applicable in some circumstances.

The length of time between each sample is also decided in advance and may be 10, 15, 20 minutes or more.

These are the kinds of decisions that need to be taken before starting the observation:

- What is the total length of time available?
- How long do you propose to spend actually observing?
- How long should there be between each observation?

It is really important to stick rigidly to your plan or the observation could become weighted towards your preferences. Remember that you need to be objective, recording accurately and factually what actually occurs.

Choosing to observe one particular aspect, for example communication, through speech also requires a degree of self-discipline.

Technique TIME SAMPLING

Description and examples of use

- takes place at fixed intervals over a period of time decided in advance
- may be used with one child, perhaps if there is concern over relationships
- may be used to estimate use of certain equipment

Necessary equipment

- pre-arranged schedule which is adhered to strictly
- pencil

Advantages

- an accurate picture about what a child is doing can be built up
- one aspect (for example, of behaviour) can be studied

Disadvantages

- pre-arranged schedule must be adhered to (if not your own preferences start to emerge!)
- if one aspect of behaviour is to be observed it is difficult to ignore everything else

Points to consider

- seek permission to observe
- how much total time is available?
- how long will each individual observation last?
- how much time will there be between each observation?

Technique EVENT SAMPLING

Description and examples of use

- records an event as it happens
- usually recorded over as long a period of time as possible
- event to be observed is decided in advance

Necessary equipment

- pen
- paper
- watch

Advantages

- useful for recording particular circumstances or positive or negative behaviour
- useful as a basis for forward planing
- useful for observing one child

Disadvantages

- difficult to observe a group of children

Points to consider

- seek permission to observe
- is this technique going to help you find out exactly what you need to know?
- how will you ensure that you are able to observe the event each time it occurs?

Technique LANGUAGE TAPE SAMPLING

Description and examples of use

- used when children are working on pre-structured tasks
- used during screening programmes in Child Health clinics

Necessary equipment

- pen
- prepared form

Advantages

- easy to use
- minimum time needed
- easy to read

Disadvantages

- may produce a rather narrow picture of the child
- it may not be recognised in a particular setting

Points to consider

- seek permission to observe
- several techniques of observing should be used to gain an overall picture of a child
- how will you bring analysis and discussion into the process?

Technique CHECKLISTS

Description and examples of use

- a list of points about child development, providing a developmental guide
- a list of points which may emphasise one aspect of child development
- used in Child Health clinics. Example of parent-held records are given on pages 73 to 75
- 'Playladders' is a checklist and is described in this chapter
- used as 'norms of reference' against which a child's development progress can be measured

Necessary equipment

- a checklist which has been planned in advance and referenced from what is acknowledged
- pencil

Advantages

- a quick way to identify developmental progress
- may identify strengths and weaknesses
- may identify exceptional ability
- easy technique to learn
- recording is easy

Disadvantages

- results may be relied on in isolation
- advanced and careful planning is necessary
- best results achieved if a good knowledge of the child exists
- best results achieved if adult is familiar to the child

Points to consider

- seek permission to observe

Technique LONGITUDINAL STUDY	

Description and examples of use

- study takes place over a longer period of time – perhaps a year or more
- a fairly full description usually given
- useful for studying progress made by child
- develops understanding of child development
- helpful for observing children with disabilities when a long-term strategy is needed

Necessary equipment

- pen
- pad

Advantages

- provides an opportunity for a general understanding of development

Disadvantages

- time burden can be too great
- unforeseen circumstances may interrupt the study

Points to consider

- seek permission to observe
- where will you conduct the study?
- what form will your notes take?

- what do you hope to achieve?
- avoid stereotyping

Technique TARGET CHILD	

Description and examples of use

- often used when there is a concern about a child or if there is a particular focus of interest
- often used to focus on concentration spans
- developed as part of the Oxford Pre-school Research Project (1970). It is a pre-coded way of collecting data

Necessary equipment

- pre-coded sheet
- pen

Advantages

- provides a focused example of a child's behaviour

Disadvantages

- you would need to learn and practise the use of each code before putting it into action

Points to consider

- seek permission
- you need to consider if you have the time to learn the codes before observing the child

Technique THE WRITTEN ACCOUNT

Description and examples of use

- written in present tense
- written to a set format
- written record of events
- written record of structured events

Necessary equipment

- notebooks
- pencils

Advantages

- good method to start with
- little preparation
- easy to learn

Disadvantages

- result may be repetitious
- you need to learn how to write down key points

Points to consider

- seek permission to observe
- decide in advance what to observe to avoid writing everything down

- you may need to develop your own shorthand

Technique DIARIES

Description and examples of use

- often used on a daily basis
- can be added to as you carry out your work
- often used to record developmental changes
- useful for studying child development

Necessary equipment

- book/pad, dated
- pen

Advantages

- useful when detailed information over a period of time is required

Disadvantages

- this method needs to be chosen with care because of the time commitment
- this method of recording can easily become biased or unreliable

Points to consider

- seek permission
- will you have regular contact with the child/children?

- how much information do you wish to record?

Technique ANECDOTAL RECORDS

Description and examples of use	Necessary equipment
• focus is usually on a particular behaviour or event which may occur intermittently • may be used as important learning experiment for you • useful for statistical purposes • useful for case studies	• notebooks • pencil

Advantages	Disadvantages
• useful for gathering information in an easy manner • useful for statistics	• anecdotal records do not offer the same continuity as diaries • it is important to avoid recording opinions

Points to consider

- seek permission
- do you need to know how frequently any 'noteworthy' behaviour occurs?
- are you trying to establish a possible reason for a child's learning style?

Technique RUNNING RECORDS: PHOTOGRAPHS, VIDEOS, CASSETTE TAPES

Description and examples of use	Necessary equipment
• written descriptions of a child's behaviour • an immediate record of what a child says or does, in sequence • photographs; reel of continuous photographs – video; audio recording • used for demonstrating a particular skill • use to supplement other observational material • may help analyse behaviour or identify special needs • may help to analyse practice	• camera • video camera • cassette tapes (audio and video) • equipment for playback

Advantages	Disadvantages
• have a range of uses • may help to confirm findings obtained through other observational methods, as tends to be unbiased • straightforward to use	• not possible to retain anonymity • evaluation should only be undertaken alongside other observational recordings • may be lengthy

Points to consider

- seek permission to photograph, video or audio record on tape from child/parent/carers
- gain agreement of staff that this is a beneficial method to use

Technique TRAIL/MOVEMENT RECORDS

Description and examples of use

- trail records give a lot of information in a shortened format. They can provide on one page information which may take three pages to write
- can be used to demonstrate use of space by one child or all the children
- useful in analysing plan of room/space and equipment

Necessary equipment

- preformatted chart
- pencil/pen

Advantages

- helps identify child's/children's needs by watching their use of space
- helps identify accessibility of equipment and how frequently used
- helps identify safety issues in the space used by the children

Disadvantages

- needs to be used with other methods of observing for in-depth analysis
- results may be of limited use

Points to consider

- you may need to design a chart
- decide how you wish to record findings
- do you need plan of room/space

■ WAYS OF REPRESENTING DATA

Technique PIE CHARTS, BAR CHARTS AND GRAPHS

Description and examples of use

- pictorial representation of information
- often used to collect data for reporting purposes

Necessary equipment

- pre-drafted chart
- pencil/pen

Advantages

- information gathered is clearly presented
- efficient method
- provides good information about groups of children

Disadvantages

- does not tend to provide sufficient information for individual children

Points to consider

- seek permission

CHAPTER SIX *Activity*

Aim: To help you understand a possible use of time sampling

Choose a child who appears to be experiencing difficulty in managing or sustaining relationships.

Decide:

■ how frequently you wish to observe (for example, every ten minutes)
■ how long each period of the observation will last (for example, two minutes).

Use the chart below to help you.

Time	Place	What is happening?	With whom?	Record any speech

Select one pre-school child from a group setting to observe at five-minute intervals for one hour. Describe the emotions you observe (fear, anger, joy, sadness, etc.). State why you think these are the emotions, and describe the circumstances surrounding the emotional state.

Use the chart below to help you.

Time	Name the emotion	Describe behaviour	Describe circumstances

Now make an asssessment of your observations and consider recommendations.
Consider your personal learning.
Write a bibliography.

Event sampling

This is a method of recording an event at the moment it happens.

The event or behaviour to be observed is decided in advance. Therefore the number of times the event occurs is recorded, when it occurs and for how long.

Event sampling may not be the best technique to use when working with a group of children. You might find yourself working with the child when the event occurs which could make the recording of it quite difficult!

This technique is useful for recording in certain circumstances, for example:

- particular behaviours demonstrated by a child with special needs
- the frequency of nightmares
- the frequency of temper tantrums
- aggressive behaviour such as biting, hitting
- poor self-control
- destructive behaviour
- the behaviours which may be exhibited by a child with diabetes mellitus particularly if you think the child's blood sugar is low
- a child's emerging skills of independence
- demonstration of acts of empathy and sympathy towards others.

There may be examples of behaviour with particular causal effects and of concern to parents or workers in early years care and education. This makes planned and accurate recording very important, the results of which may require prompt action.

Event sampling is particularly useful as part of a range of observation methods which together give breadth and depth to the overall picture of the child.

CHAPTER SIX *Activity*

Aim: To help you understand a possible way use of event sampling

Choose a child who you have noticed is showing destructive behaviour. Decide when this destructive behaviour is to be observed, for example over one day, three days or one week.

Use the chart below to help you.

Time	Event No.	Length of time	Description

Now make an assessment and consider recommendations.

Consider your personal learning and any recommendations. Make references to texts you have read.

Write a bibliography.

Language tape sampling

Language tape sampling will enable you to examine a child's speech closely. It is an effective way of preserving useful information for meaning and analysis. You will need to obtain permission from the child's parents.

Setting up a tape recorder in a placement must be done with care. You need to ensure that the tape recorder is not visible so that the child is unaware that a recording is taking place. This will ensure a natural response from the child. However, the microphone cannot be too far away or the quality of sound will be poor.

This is a technique worth developing, particularly when you are looking at language development or if you are monitoring a child who has speech and language delay.

When you have the opportunity you could discuss with the speech and language therapist the results of your observations and assessments. Your results may help the team plan ahead for the child's needs.

Checklists

These are best used with children you know well. They can be used to monitor developmental progress. They may be particularly helpful in identifying areas where special support is needed, for example if a child is experiencing fine manipulation difficulties. 'Playladders' is an example of a checklist and can be found on page 65.

Longitudinal study

This is a study which is carried out over a much longer period of time, perhaps even a year or more.

It will enable you to observe the progress made by a child in certain areas of development. A student on a course may study a baby in a family. Discussing the child's progress with the family can be beneficial as this gives additional insight into the child's development and progress. This method may be helpful in observing children with special needs where a long-term strategy is needed.

Target child

This method involves observing the child at regular, pre-arranged intervals. It is a pre-coded way of collecting data so you would need to learn and practise the use of each code before putting it into action.

Recording your observation

Use a ready drawn-up recording sheet (see the example on page 59). Have a watch, preferably with a second hand, so that you can record minute by minute. Observe for several minutes before you start to write anything down.

Write down what the child does in each minute in the Activity column. For example, 'Pulls small lump off large piece of dough, squeezes it, watches child opposite.' Write down exactly what happens without adding any interpretation. Also jot down a note about the activity and materials and whether other children or adults are present. For example, 'Table with 2 large lumps of blue dough, 2 other children, helper sitting there.'

Write down what the child says and what other children or adults say to him, for each minute, in the Language column. It is often impossible to write down the exact words spoken, but record the gist of comments if you can.

It is helpful to use the following abbreviations as a sort of short-hand to help you note down quickly what is done and said:

TC	target child (the child you are observing)
C	other child
A	any adult (staff member, mother-helper, teenage student, the observer (you))
→	speaks to

These abbreviations are especially useful in noting the language. Here are some examples:

TC	sings to self
TC→C:	'I'm the father and you're the mother.'
C→TC:	'You're not coming to my birthday party.'
A→TC:	comforts him
TC→A:	'Will you tie my apron please?'
TC→C	conversation
TC unison	sings
A→Group	announces milk-time
A→TC+C	reads a story

Note: The Language column does not include instances where the child is listening to another conversation without participating or being included. This would be written down in the Activity column.

If you are interrupted for a short time whilst observing, don't worry. Just note it as an 'interruption'.

After your observation is finished, make a note of what the child does next. This may help you to make better sense of what he was doing at the end of the observation.

The following pages show a completed Target Child observation.

The written account, on-the-spot record or specimen record

This method is often referred to as 'free description'. It is likely to be one of the first methods you try. It allows you to record events or structured activities as they happen. It is written in the present tense and thus provides a lively account of what is happening. You must remember to be objective in your recording and only write what you see and hear. An example of this method is given at the end of Chapter 5, page 42.

Diaries

Diaries can be used, probably on a daily basis, as you carry out your work with the children. You can record developmental changes, group or individual changes. The method may be useful where detailed information over a period of time is required. A diary ensures that the observation not only takes the child into account but also more fully the context of the child's environment. It may therefore contain features of other methods, such as anecdotal records and running records, examples of which follow.

The diary method needs to be chosen with care because of the time commitment necessary. Particular care must be taken to ensure accurate and objective observations are recorded. This method of recording can easily become subjective, biased and unreliable.

TARGET CHILD – SPONTANEOUS OBSERVATION
AIM

My aim was to observe a child's spontaneous behaviour over a period of 10 minutes using the Target Child Method.

PLANNING

I obtained the permission of the pre-school leader to carry on a series of observations of which this is an example.

It is a spontaneous observation of a child, whose initials are R.P., playing at the dough table together with another child.

The child was chosen at random. I elected to pick the third child through the door that morning.

RATIONALE

This method of observation was produced in 1979 by the Oxford Pre-School Research Project. It is a systematic guide to narrative observation of children at play and as it focused on the activity of a single child, it became known as the 'Target Child' System.

This method enables the observer to record and analyse lengthy and complicated material quickly and systematically, giving a brief picture of a child's behaviour in 10 minutes. It can also be shared with other child care professionals who are familiar with the system.

The reason for using this method is that once the observation has been completed, it can then give access to the following information:

- it shows the level of a child's skills, whom the child talks to, for what reason and how;
- the themes/activities the child chooses and length of time the child sustains them;
- levels of interaction with other children and adults, whether they initiate it or merely respond;
- areas where the child shows competence or where there might be some delay;
- the preoccupations of a child, whether seeking stories, conversations, make-believe play or following through an intellectual concept of something being 'inside' or 'underneath'.

The Target Child Method can also be used for activity-based observations. These observations are useful for a group wishing to ensure that their provision is achieving its aim. The observations can reveal the following:

- the kinds of play and learning most often promoted by the activity;
- the amount and types of conversation it produces;
- whether adult presence makes a difference to play and conversation;
- whether the activity sustains long stretches of play linked to a single theme or to short 'one-off' actions;
- what fires and keeps children's interest and concentration, and also what brings them to an end.

With this information gained, it enables a group not only to make changes if necessary, but also to monitor the effects of change.

PRINCIPLES OF TARGET CHILD METHOD

I offer the attached completed sheet of a spontaneous observation to demonstrate my understanding of the principles of the Target Child Method.

PERSONAL LEARNING

From this observation I have personally learnt that Playdough™ is one of the more expressive materials available for the children to play with.

Children want to explore and experiment with it, they want to know what they can actually do with it. Younger children firstly explore it by feeling and seeing it change shape. Older children, such as the Target Child, finally realise that the shape they have made is a model. Whatever the age of the child, all seem to enjoy the sensations that playing with Playdough™ can give.

Dough can be used in a creative, imaginative way, and in an aggressive way for emotional release. It can also give pleasure by being soothing and relaxing to the user. It also lends itself for pretend play, e.g. cake making/domestic play providing a link between home and pre-school.

Playdough™ enhances manipulative skills and small muscle movement. The Target Child demonstrated her manipulative skills by rolling, cutting, pressing and breaking the dough, together with her use of the implements and equipment.

This activity helps sensory development. The children learn to explore the material and its properties. They also learn about texture and shapes. Dough play helps with basic science and mathematical learning, such as size and capacity. The Target Child was breaking off small amounts of dough and squeezing it into a 6-hole cake tin showing that she knew that by pressing down she would ultimately get more dough into the hole. As the Playdough™ is a different colour each week, this also reinforces the learning of colours. Children learn from activities which have a specific end, i.e. making something out of dough.

Creative activities provide excellent opportunities for conversations between children and this was clearly shown in my observation. As the Target Child used the equipment provided with the Playdough™, this in turn generated conversation, which was of a high level.

This activity can release tensions and emotions. The Target Child was pressing down hard using her knuckles and thumbs as she played with the dough. This emotion was also portrayed on her face as she gritted her teeth. There was also much pleasure gained by the two girls from this activity especialy when the Target Child snatched a cutter from her friend and hid it in a bowl. This resulted in squeals of laughter from them both.

Dough play helps broaden social experiences which was again demonstrated in the observation. There was good interaction between the Target Child and her friend. They actually played together in 'co-operative' play.

I therefore conclude that this activity helps develop the child in a number of areas. It sustains children's attention for long stretches and encourages social, emotional, intellectual and language development.

EQUAL OPPORTUNITIES

The Equal Opportunities Policy in my group is: To treat every child with the utmost respect and consideration, to ensure that no child is ever discriminated against for any reason. They also welcome children with special needs.

This activity is clearly suitable for all children whatever religion, culture or gender. It can easily be adapted for children with special needs say, if a child were in a wheelchair, a tray could be attached on the side. The activity could also be carried out at a more suitable table whereby a wheelchair could fit underneath. Gloves can be worn if children have a skin complaint.

FIGURE 6.1B *A completed Target Child Observation*

SPONTANEOUS OBSERVATION

Child's initials: R.P.   Sex: F   Age: 3 yrs   Date and time observed 16.10.95
                                          7 mths   11.10 am

Minutes	Activity record	Language record	Task	Social
1.	T.C. Picks up dough in right hand rolls between hands. Puts it on table and rolls dough into long sausage. Picks up a spoon in right hand, using handle makes indentation. Presses two ends together to form circle and places on head.	MAN	PAIR/SG	
2.	T.C. Cutting up dough into small strips with right hand. Using left hand, picks up pieces together and places on a plate.	T.C.: 'I need a knife.' Child 1: 'You have that knife.'	MAN	PAIR
3.	T.C. Reaches across table and grabs a 6 hole cake tin. Breaks off dough and presses into holes using left thumb.	Child 1: 'Don't break it off, do this.'	MAN	PAIR
4.	T.C. Rolls out more dough into long roll. Bends it into arch with both hands. Picks up shape cutter with right hand, puts dough around it.	T.C.: 'He has a green face.'	MAN	PAIR
5.	Adult walks over to dough table. T.C. looks up at adult and points to child 1 standing next to her.	Adult: 'Where's Hattie?' Adult: 'You haven't had your photo taken, Rebecca did.' Child 1: 'No!'	WA	PAIR
6.	T.C. wanders off. She heads straight over to photographer & watches what is going on.		WA	SOL/SG
7.	T.C. returns to dough table. Stands next to child 1. T.C. stretches over table to collect more dough & knocks small oven off table onto floor	T.C.: 'Oh no!" Child 1: 'We need that.'	PM	PAIR/SG
8.	Adult comes back to table. T.C. is putting large lump of dough into small bowl, pressing down with right knuckle.	A: 'Hattie please. Your mother' would like a photo taken.' T.C. Singing Pat a Cake Song.	MAN	PAIR/SG
9.	Child 2 Strolls up. T.C. rolls dough out with rolling pin. Selects cutter in right hand presses down on dough with both hands. Peels away dough from around cutter.	T.C. 'We are making a birthday cake.' Child 2: 'Whose birthday is it?' T.C.: 'Your birthday.'	MAN	PAIR/SG
10.	T.C. Snatches cutter being used by child 1 with right hand. Places it under lid of bowl containing dough. T.C. then opens & shuts the lid in quick succession.	Child 1: 'I was using that one.' T.C.: 'Abracadabra.' Child 1: 'I want it.' T.C.: 'Abracadabra.' (Squeals of laughter from them both.)	PM	PAIR

SPONTANEOUS OBSERVATION
Child's initials: Sex: Age: Date and time observed

Minutes	Activity record	Language record	Task	Social
1.				
2.				
3.				
4.				
5.				
6.				
7.				
8.				
9.				
10.				

Anecdotal records

You can use anecdotal records to focus on a particular behaviour or event which may occur intermittently. Anecdotes do not offer the same continuity as diaries, but you may judge that some noteworthy behaviour needs observing. This may provide an important learning experience for you.

This method can be useful for statistical purposes and case studies.

Anecdotal recording can be useful in gathering information which may help to establish:

- frequency of 'noteworthy' behaviour
- possible reason for a child's behaviour
- possible reason for a child's learning style
- feedback about what a child might have learned
- what circumstances may reinforce a child's behaviour.

Running records

Running records are written descriptions of a child's behaviour. They offer immediate records of what the child says or does, in sequence. There are various ways you can make running records:

- by using words
- audio tapes
- videos
- photographs
- sketches
- sociograms
- diagrams.

This type of record can help you and others reflect on the past, focus on the present and plan for the future.

The running record is a popular method and will provide you with a sound foundation in observing, from which you can branch out into alternative methods.

Helpful hint

It is a good idea to devise your own 'shorthand' codes so that you can swiftly record what is happening. You need to find codes with which you are happy. Here are a few ideas to start off:

+	= and	Rs	= runs
A	= adult/carer	LH	= left hand
Ws	= walks	RH	= right hand

Trail/movement record

Trail or movement records can provide a substantial amount of information in an easily accessible manner.

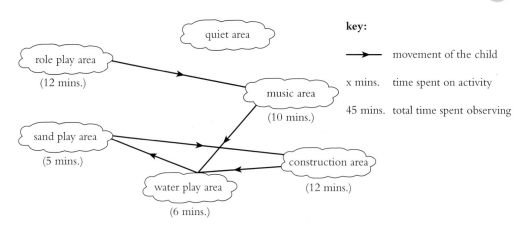

FIGURE 6.3 *An example of a Trail/Movement Record*

Trail records can help to identify a child's use of equipment within the workplace, or monitor safety issues.

A trail record can be helpful when planning the use of resources within a given area. The end result could look like this:

WAYS OF REPRESENTING DATA COLLECTED DURING OBSERVATIONS

Pie and bar charts and graphs

These are pictorial representations of collected data and are constructed after the observation or observations.

They provide clear, accessible information about groups of children but do not tend to provide sufficient information about individual children.

Here is an example of a pie chart following observations of twenty four-year-old children using scissors. The data collected could also be represented in the form of a bar chart.

An example of a percentile graph is given on page 74.

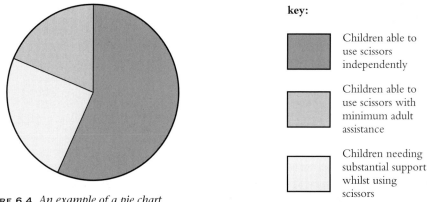

FIGURE 6.4 *An example of a pie chart*

■ EXAMPLES OF RECORD KEEPING: OTHER METHODS

It is a good idea to have a look at different systems of record keeping so that you can make comparisons. Records can show a fuller picture of a child by building up information shared between home and professionals. Records can demonstrate a child's strengths and a child's self-assessment can form an important part of these records. The child could be videoed or taped talking about his or her achievements or an adult can act as a scribe for the child. Parental consent is necessary and many records are held by parents.

High Scope

High Scope have developed an ongoing system of observation and assessment identifying key experiences which are central to a young child's development. These experiences are about what children do naturally. High Scope has described these key experiences as:

- creative representation
- language and literacy
- initiative and social relations
- movement
- music
- classification
- seriation
- number
- space
- time

The key experiences are used as the basis for the High Scope record keeping process.

The Child Observation Record (COR) is an observational tool designed to be used by adults working with children in everyday activities. Staff complete the COR based on observations they record as children are playing, building, exploring, pretending, solving problems – in short, doing all of the things children do in normal activity. The COR assesses child development in the areas listed above. In the High Scope approach careful observation of children's activity is seen as central to planning and teaching.

The observation record is in keeping with the underlying beliefs which recognise children's abilities to become independent active learners.

For further advice on High Scope please contact: High Scope UK, 190–192 Maple Road, London, SE20 8HT.

Quality control

High Scope stresses these three points in order to maintain quality in practice:

- First you need to know the child quite well.
- The observation sheet must not be administered as a test.
- There is a strong emphasis on building upon the child's strengths not weaknesses.

CHILD: Victoria
OBSERVER: Malek/Ruth

HIGH/SCOPE KEY EXPERIENCE NOTE FORM

CREATIVE REPRESENTATION	LANGUAGE & LITERACY	INITIATIVE & SOCIAL RELATIONS	MOVEMENT	MUSIC
12/5 - During WT, put her two feet into plastic blocks and sliding said," Look, look I'm skiing."	20/5 - At WT in the reading area retold the story of "Three little pigs" turning the correct pages.	10/5 - When Charlotte ran and fell down Victoria rushed to help her up and brushed her tears with a tissue.	19/6 - Threw and caught a bean bag four times without dropping it during OT.	20/6 - At WT lined up the children in the music area and made them sing Nursery rhymes while she conducted with a wooden spoon.
17/6 - Playing in the HA, dressed as a mum, took a mop and mopped the floor.	3/6 - At PT traced her name on the planning sheet.	20/5 - Helped John with his coat at OT.	22/6 - Suggested that all the children walk like an elephant to the planning area from Greeting circle.	16/6 - Arranged pots and cups on the table. Then using a spoon hit each one in turn and said, "I'm making music."
23/6 - At SGT put different coloured tissue papers on the glue on a piece of paper and said to Josie," I've made a big bonfire."	29/6 - In the dressing-up area of the HA talking to Vicky said, "'I'm so tired! I've had a busy day. When I was putting the baby to bed, the phone rang. It was granny from Ireland. Just then the TV man came to repair the TV. Then daddy wanted his tea early!"	9/6 - At WT, cleaned up the table and put away the glue and collage materials before moving on to the next activity.	30/6 - Climbed up and down the climbing frame without holding on to the bar on the side.	
			3/7 - Drew around different sized circles and cut around them.	

CLASSIFICATION	SERIATION	NUMBER	SPACE	TIME
5/7 - During CT touched my hair and said, "Your hair's black but mine's blonde."	2/5 - Whilst playing in the small toys area arranged laces from longest to shortest.	2/6 - Gave each child a cup and a serviette at snack time and said," there's 3 left".	18/5 - During snack time said, "I want the biscuit in "the middle".	29/6 - Said, " my birthday is at Christmas time."
13/7 - At tidy up time found a piece of lego with the beads and said "This does not belong here."	15/5 - Using different sized star cutters cut biscuits from rolled dough. Then placing them in order from largest to smallest said," This one (pointing to largest) is the daddy one. This one (middle size) is the mummy one and this one (smallest) is the baby one".	21/6 - At dough table, rolled dough, cut 5 cookies and counted 1, 2, 3, 4, 5.	24/5 - Looking through a box of old envelopes found one big enough to put her picture in, without folding.	6/7 - Said, " My mum says I'm going to the big school in September."
18/7 - At SGT sorted all the buttons by size and then sorted shells by texture.	26/5 - Standing by James said, I'm bigger than you cause I'm taller."	28/6 - Counted the children in the HA. Then went shopping with her doll and came back with a lollipop for each of the 4 children.	14/6 - Guessed how many cookies she could cut from the rolled dough. Then carefully started to cut these.	17/7 - Said that she would give John a turn on the bike in two minutes and did so shortly without being reminded.

MP/HS UK '95

FIGURE 6.5 *An example of High Scope Key Experience Note Form*

In-depth discussion

In a setting using High Scope an adult team had observed and recorded over a three-week period that a three-and-a-half-year-old girl was exploring telephones and using them extensively in her play. It was a self-choice activity. The team decided to follow up this child's interest by introducing telephones as a planning strategy for this child in the High Scope 'Plan, Do and Review' sequence.

Think of a similar situation where a child is showing a particular interest. How might you plan to foster this interest?

Playladders

This is a method of observing how children play and it is intended to help children achieve the next step on the ladder. Playladders can be used flexibly as the material can be adapted to suit a variety of settings.

Playladders are obtainable from Hannah Mortimer, Ainderby Hall, Northallerton, North Yorkshire, DL7 9QJ.

Record keeping in a nursery school

The following example of record keeping was developed by a nursery school in Croydon. This process relies upon skilled, accurate observations and assessments. (See Figure 6.7.)

This is the school's broad-based plan and shows the important part which observations and assessments play in curriculum planning.

Each child has a diary sheet on which teaching staff can enter relevant information, preliminary visit notes and medical information. Family births and/or deaths are also recorded together with any other information which may have an influence on the child's performance in school.

When the parent or carer attends a preliminary visit at the end of the summer term staff 'talk through' the Home Visit Booklet. Parents or carers then take the booklet away with them and it is used as an 'ice breaker' during the home visit. Staff take a box of various items to play with children and record the child's reactions and behaviour on the Home Visit Observation Sheet.

Observation record sheet

Two children are observed during each morning and afternoon session. All staff focus on two children. They have notebooks with them the whole time. Notes are entered onto the Observation Record Sheet.

Fridays are used to catch up on those children who may have been absent on their timetabled day.

Each Friday lunchtime all staff meet to discuss the sixteen children who were observed the previous week. Decisions are made about strategies for each child to enable further development.

Each child's observation sheet has previously completed observation sheets clipped directly behind to compare progress. All entries on observation sheets are dated and initialled by staff and all strategies are entered on the observation sheet. Lists of the strategies are copied for the observation file and planning file.

playladders

name:
nursery area: LARGE SPACE
play activity: TRICYCLE/CAR

step	repertoire	✓
3	Pedals freely and quickly Able to manoeuvre around obstacles Plays in a game with other children Links with other activities e.g. dressing up, delivering, organising passengers etc.	
2	Turns corners Makes bell sound/hooter/engine noises Pedals for short distances Avoids collision	
1	Listens and joins in if adult pretends they are in a car etc. Moves along using feet to push with Pushes to and fro by using feet Sits in/on and allows adult to push it.	

playladders

name:
nursery area: LARGE SPACE
play activity: CLIMBING FRAME

step	repertoire	✓
3	Climbs all over Can balance with "no hands" Manages ladder without help Hangs from higher bars Seems aware of dangers, and can warn other children Combines in other play e.g. "all aboard" a ship Can repeat sequences of three actions	
2	Climbs up Jumps down about 8" Climbs a few steps up the ladder Waits for other children to move out of way	
1	Climbs through bottom bars Jumps down about 4" Climbs down with help Climbs onto lower bars (may need lifting off) Hangs from lower bars Watches others with interest	

FIGURE 6.6 *Playladders*

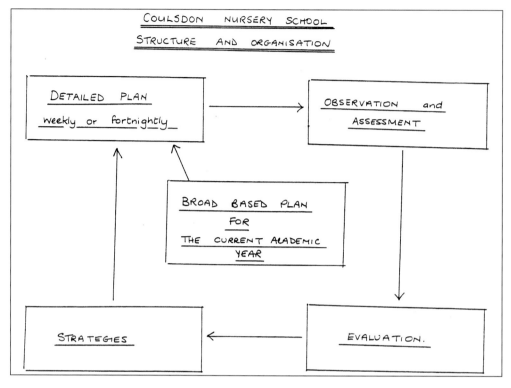

FIGURE 6.7 *Record keeping in a nursery school*

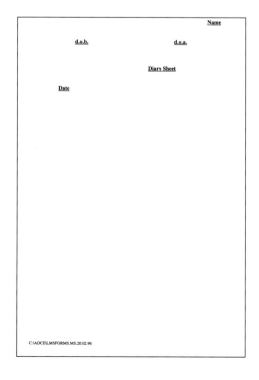

FIGURE 6.8 *Diary sheet*

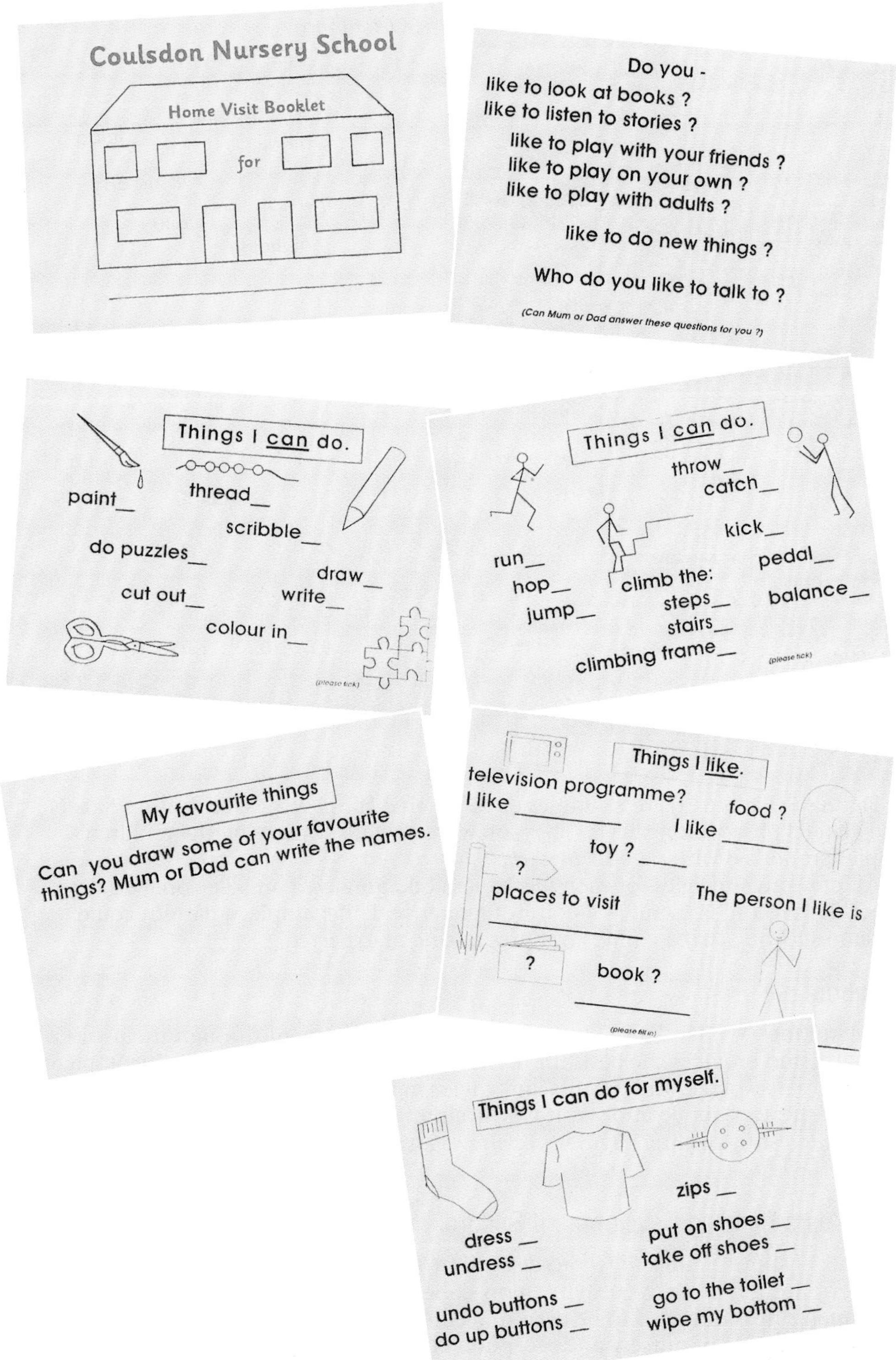

Coulsdon Nursery School

Home Visit Booklet

for

Do you -
like to look at books ?
like to listen to stories ?
like to play with your friends ?
like to play on your own ?
like to play with adults ?

like to do new things ?

Who do you like to talk to ?

(Can Mum or Dad answer these questions for you ?)

Things I **can** do.

paint__
thread__
scribble__
do puzzles__
draw__
cut out__   write__
colour in__

(please tick)

Things I **can** do.

throw__
catch__
kick__
run__
hop__   climb the: pedal__
jump__   steps__   balance__
stairs__
climbing frame__   (please tick)

My favourite things

Can you draw some of your favourite
things? Mum or Dad can write the names.

Things I **like**.

television programme?
I like _____   food ?
I like __
toy ? __
?
places to visit   The person I like is

?   book ?
_____

(please fill in)

Things I can do for myself.

zips __
dress __   put on shoes __
undress __   take off shoes __

undo buttons __   go to the toilet __
do up buttons __   wipe my bottom __

FIGURE 6.9 *Home visit booklet*

Books
Spot – good handling looked at it herself. Named the animals.

COULSDON NURSERY SCHOOL
Home Visit – Observation Record Sheet
Date: 8/9/99   Name: M —

Others present: Dog Barney   Dad Mum babysitter
Will extra support be needed?

Signed:

Puzzles
Need some direction. When wrong said 'silly me' 9 set – easily done

Pens / Pencils / Paper
Right tripod hold good arth-hold little lines on the paper – may be new to her (pens)

Scissors
Right correct hold. Can cut

Threading toy
easily done but not for long

Soft toy / Puppet
liked the puppet took it for a ride in her basket on her new bike

Own "home" toys
new bike with stabilisers hair set doll covers Park

Conversation / Speech
good language & vocabulary. asks lots of questions Told me about her pond cake with 2 ducks non-stop talking

Other general comments
very friendly Birthday yesterday Recognised 'm' in the book as the same that starts her name. JJ very small in size

FIGURE 6.10 *Home Visit Observation Record Sheet*

Figures 6.9 and 6.10 are examples of completed Home Visit Observation Sheets and general observation sheets. They are written whilst observing the children. Copies are shared with parents or carers.

All previous strategies for each particular child are saved on a Personal Strategy Sheet. This record is useful as a point of reference. For example, a pattern could develop showing that a child is not progressing as expected.

'All about me'

'All about me' (Wolfendale, 1990) is a record of development through the use of a checklist, and provides the basis for discussion on a child's progress. It is completed by early years workers and parents and covers many aspects of a child's development between the ages of two and six. It is written in the first person and thus makes lively, interesting reading. Figure 6.13 shows an example from the 'All about me' record.

Early Years Reading Development Record

Figure 6.14 shows a nursery record devised by Croydon Advisory Service. A nursery record of this nature draws heavily upon skilled observations and subsequent assessments. It is intended to be used to record the development of individual children's reading in nursery and reception classes and to provide information for future planning. Statements in the Record can be highlighted, ticked and initialled.

Social Development	COULSDON NURSERY SCHOOL
Independent in what she is going to do in her 'play'. 12/5 Solitary play this morning 12/5	**Observation Record Sheet** Date: 12 May 99 Name: A—— **Agreed strategy for further development:** Promote her love of songs and music by involving her in using cassette tape – maybe to record her own voice. Praise her for good attention span during storytime sessions.

Response to Learning 6/6	Mathematical Concepts 12/5	Creative Arts
Knew the names of all the animals she had painted. Really enjoys having a little joke with an adult. Is able to follow adults' suggestions to extend her drawings	Draws a butterfly in a symmetrical way, thus: Drew O today and asked me 'Is it a circle?'	Very interested in the farm shop. 5.9 Enjoys playdough – also made a snowman with a hat, eyes, nose etc. Listened to taped music and enjoys performing. Joins in singing and music making. Sang 'Bingo' with group at storytime, yet did not understand about verses with pauses.

Communication Skills	Processes in Science	Gross Motor Skills
Initiates conversations much more readily with me now. Asks adults many questions from which she seeks reassurance.	Talks about the insects in her garden – draws them well, describes and names them accurately. Relates her butterfly drawing to a story she has read about 'Very Hungry Caterpillar'	Running is slightly clumsy. Good balance with scooter, pushing with right foot. Happy about sharing garden top with others. Is able to roll (unaided) down the garden inside the blue barrel. Pedals big trike fast.

Early Writing and Reading	Technology	Fine Motor Skills
Limited concentration during storytime. Writes freely L→R using numbers & letter shapes written between lines that she draws. Reads back what she writes. Good concentration while writing. Uses her finger to scan beneath words when reading.	Interested in using the cassette recorder. Very interested in the computer but needs adult support or interest goes. Identifies and remembers words on computer screen. Good use of computer controls	Drew a lovely picture of 2 butterflies each with 4 sections & spots – each had feelers. Later made a 3D b/fly using playdough & plastic shapes. R-H with correct pencil grip.

Desktop Publishing Reprographics Unit Schools Advisory Service   (Observation Sheet)

FIGURE 6.11 *Observation Record Sheet*

COULSDON NURSERY SCHOOL

Observation Record Sheet

Date: _____   Name: _____

Agreed strategy for further development:

1.   Lots of encouragement and praise when she gets involved with activities.

2.   Adult to engage A..... in conversation. Can she talk about what she is doing?

COULSDON NURSERY SCHOOL

Observation Record Sheet

Date: _____   Name: _____

Agreed strategy for further development:

Strategies discussed with S: 31/10/95

Encourage daily visits to graphics area.
Practice fine motor skills
Colour recognition

COULSDON NURSERY SCHOOL

Observation Record Sheet

Date: _____   Name: _____

Agreed strategy for further development:

Praise her when she actually completes a task on her own. e.g. jigsaws.

Frequently ask her what she is doing/has been doing/is going to do next. Make
eye contact with her and insist that she responds to you - verbally.

95

FIGURE 6.12 *Personal Strategy Sheet*

Hold a conversation with other people about such things as

_____

Tell people about things, such as

_____

Carry out a request or instruction, such as

_____

What else can I say?

_____

What we already do at home to help my language

_____

What we can do in future to help my language to develop

_____

We speak more than one language at home. They are

_____

How am I getting on?   **comments**
_____

Do we have any worries
about my development
and progress?

☐ some   ☐ no

_____

Some plans and hopes my family might have for me for the next few months or for
the future

FIGURE 6.13 *An example from 'All about me'*

Record Keeping, Health

See Figure 6.15 for examples of the parent-held records used in an NHS Trust.

OTHER METHODS OF OBSERVING AND REPRESENTING DATA

Other methods of observing and ways of representing data exist. You may find that different terminology is used. For further reading refer to Bartholomew and Bruce (1993) and Webb (1981).

EARLY YEARS READING DEVELOPMENT RECORD

Name:

Languages spoken:

SCHOOLS ADVISORY SERVICE — CROYDON

Raising Standards (Hodder & Stoughton)

ATTITUDE TO BOOKS AND STORIES

(i) Individually, with other children and with adults/s

Participates with interactive books.	Turns pages independently.	Turns pages accurately.	Knows front and back (according to heritage script).
Begins to retell stories.	Retells stories using story props.	Retells stories with expression.	Retells familiar stories.
Retell stories in own words.	Retells stories in heritage language.	Memorises chunks of language of own well-known books.	Retells joining in predictable structure.
Relates to own experience.	Retells, aware when own version departs from original.	Notices and self-corrects when own version departs from original.	Enjoys listening to taped stories.

(ii) Individually and with other children

Chooses to take books to and from home.	Brings own books from home.	Looks for familiar stories.	Chooses books thoughtfully.
Looks for favourite stories.	Chooses books on a familiar theme.	Chooses comforting books.	Tells stories while playing.
Tells story to self.	Reads in role.	Imitates adults.	Finds a special place to read.
Reads to friends/toys.	Concentrates for sustained periods.	Discusses books with friends.	Enjoys reading own made books.

(iii) With adults [One to one] ⟶ ⟵ [In a group]

Willing to share books with encouragement.	Responds to invitation 'Come and share a book with me/us'.	Holds book with encouragement.	Concentrates in small group story time.
Willing to hold book.	Turns pages with encouragement.	Talks about a story with encouragement.	Joins in discussion in a small group.
Comments on story.	Asks to share stories with adults.	Asks 'who wrote it?'	Joins in discussion in a large group.
Discusses a story with an adult.	Responds to 'I wonder what...?'	Asks questions during story discussion.	Concentrates in large group story time.
			Responds with enthusiasm in story sessions.

RHYTHM AND RHYME

Hums the rhythm of familiar stories.	Enjoys playing with sounds	Enjoys trying new words.	Joins in actions and movements of rhymes.
Enjoys word play.	Joins in, echoing sound patterns.	Joins in with rhymes.	Joins in echoing words.
Joins in repeated sections.	Enjoys chanting rhymes, rhythmic phrases.	Sings/tells rhymes.	Knows some rhymes by heart.
Retells, imitating sound patterns.	Retells using rhythm of text.		

READING ILLUSTRATIONS

Comments on illustration.	Mulls over illustrations.	Begins to notice detail.	Notices detail.
Identifies humour/other emotions in illustrations.	Anticipates what will happen from illustrations.	Chooses books for specific illustrations.	Reads illustrations, making connections with own experiences.
Asks questions about illustrations.	Recognises books by the cover.	Matches books illustrated by the same person.	Chooses books by specific illustrator.
Predicts content from the cover.	Retells in own language using illustrations.	Retells in book language using illustrations.	

PRINT AWARENESS

Notices print in the environment.	Notices and matches logos.	Shows interest in print of home language.	Aware of heritage scripts.
Aware of different fonts and styles.	Notices print - what does that say?	Knows print carries messages.	Interacts with print in display.
Recognises own name.	Recognises shapes of high interest letters.	Matches initial letters.	Recognises names of friends/family.
Recognises books by the print on the cover.	Recognises books by the same author	Recognises letters from names.	Finger scans left to right.
			Aware of punctuation.

LG Early Years Reading Dev.

FIGURE 6.14 *Early years reading development record*

FIGURE 6.15A

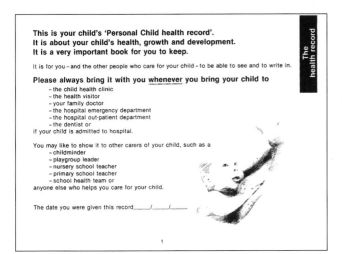

This is your child's 'Personal Child health record'.
It is about your child's health, growth and development.
It is a very important book for you to keep.

It is for you – and the other people who care for your child – to be able to see and to write in.

Please always bring it with you whenever you bring your child to
    – the child health clinic
    – the health visitor
    – your family doctor
    – the hospital emergency department
    – the hospital out-patient department
    – the dentist or
if your child is admitted to hospital.

You may like to show it to other carers of your child, such as a
    – childminder
    – playgroup leader
    – nursery school teacher
    – primary school teacher
    – school health team or
anyone else who helps you care for your child.

The date you were given this record_____/_____/_____

The health record

1

FIGURE 6.15B

This record is about
This is the 'Personal child health record' of:
● Please place a sticker (if available) otherwise write in space provided.

Surname
First names
NHS number   Local no
Address
Postcode   D.O.B.___/___/___   Sex M/F
G.P.   Code
H.V.   Code

Parents:
Mother's surname
First name
Father's surname
First name

Change of Address (including post code)
1) _____ Tel _____
2) _____ Tel _____
3) _____ Tel _____
4) _____ Tel _____

Change of Family Doctor
1) Name _____ Address _____ Tel _____
2) Name _____ Address _____ Tel _____
3) Name _____ Address _____ Tel _____
4) Name _____ Address _____ Tel _____

Change of Health Visitor
1) Name _____ Address _____ Tel _____
2) Name _____ Address _____ Tel _____
3) Name _____ Address _____ Tel _____
4) Name _____ Address _____ Tel _____

Child's details

3

FIGURE 6.15C

Birth details
● Please place a sticker (if available) otherwise write in space provided.

Surname
First names
NHS number   Local no
Address
Postcode   D.O.B.___/___   Sex M/F
G.P.   Code
H.V.   Code

Place of birth _____
Expected date of delivery___/___/___
Actual date of delivery ___/___/___
Problems during pregnancy/birth:
(1) _____
(2) _____
(3) _____
(4) _____

Birth weight_____kg.   Length (if relevant)_____cm
Head circ._____cm – Date of measurement ___/___/___
(1) Hip examination   S P O T R N _____
(2) Hip examination   S P O T R N _____
Testes   S P O T R N _____
General examination   S P O T R N _____
(S = Satisfactory; P = Problem; O = Observation; T = Treated; R = Referred; N = Not examined.
(If two or more codes seem to apply—select the last one e.g. R takes priority over T, T over O etc.)
Follow-up hospital appointment   Yes/No
Feeding at discharge   Breast/Bottle/Mixed

Blood tests done   Date___/___/___
Phenylketonuria   Yes/No   Norm/Abn
Thyroid test   Yes/No   Norm/Abn
Haemoglobinopathies   Yes/No   Norm/Abn
Comments _____

Top Yellow Copy: DHA. 2nd Green Copy: to GP/HV.
Third White Copy: stay in PCHR.

Birth details

7

FIGURE 6.15D

Your child should have the following immunisations

Age due	Immunisation	Comments	Date Given
2 months	Diphtheria/Tetanus/Whooping Cough, Polio		
	Hib		
3 months	Diphtheria/Tetanus/Whooping Cough/Polio		
	Hib		
4 months	Diphtheria/Tetanus/Whooping Cough/Polio		
	Hib		
12-18 months	Measles, Mumps, Rubella (MMR)		
3-5 years	Diphtheria, Tetanus, Polio.		
	MMR (unless already given)		
10-14 years	Heaf test and BCG (optional)		
15-18 years	Tetanus, Polio and Low Dose Diphtheria		

Other immunisations (eg BCG at birth)

1_____ Date___/___/___   4_____ Date___/___/___

2_____ Date___/___/___   5_____ Date___/___/___

3_____ Date___/___/___   6_____ Date___/___/___

Note any changes to the full course

All children should receive immunisations except a very few children who
1 are suffering from a feverish illness – when the immunisation should be postponed until full recovery
2 have had a severe reaction to a previous immunisation (see 'Help' section for mild upsets)
3 have an illness or are taking medicines that interfere with their ability to fight infections.
Children taking antibiotics can be immunised.
Before each immunisation the doctor or nurse will make sure that it is alright to give your child the vaccine.

Immunisation

9

FIGURE 6.15E

Major health problems

This page is for doctors to fill in with you. It will only be used if there is a problem.

1 _____ Date diagnosed _____
2 _____ Date diagnosed _____
3 _____ Date diagnosed _____
4 _____ Date diagnosed _____

Serious reactions to drugs

1 _____ Date diagnosed _____
2 _____ Date diagnosed _____
3 _____ Date diagnosed _____

Serious allergies

1 _____ Date diagnosed _____
2 _____ Date diagnosed _____

Look out for these 'Safety signs'
when you borrow or buy.

Medical details

5

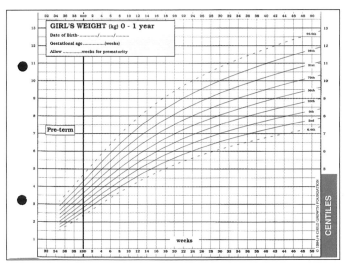

FIGURE 6.15F

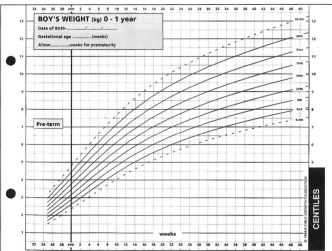

FIGURE 6.15G

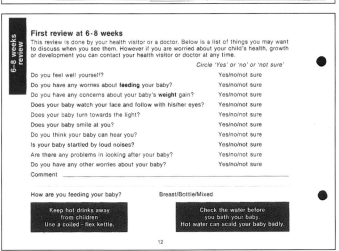

FIGURE 6.15H

FIGURE 6.15I

OXFORD

* Please place a sticker (if available) otherwise write in space provided.

Surname
First names
NHS number Local no
Sex M/F
Address
Postcode D.O.B. / /
G.P. Code
H.V. Code

Date of present contact / /
Name of Examiner
Examiner Code Number
LENGTH cm centile
WEIGHT kg centile
HEAD CIRC. cm centile

Any previous ongoing medical problems? No ☐ Yes ☐
If 'yes' please specify (1) ____ (2) ____ (3) ____

ITEM	CODE (Ring one)*	COMMENT
Physical	S P O T R N	
Vision	S P O T R N	
Hearing	S P O T R N	
Locomotion	S P O T R N	
Manipulation	S P O T R N	
Speech/Lang	S P O T R N	
Behaviour	S P O T R N	
Hips	S P O T R N	
Testes	S P O T R N	
Heart	S P O T R N	

*(If one or more codes seem to apply select the last one e.g. R takes priority over T, T over O etc.)
S = Satisfactory *(normal result)*
P = Problem *(significant condition on record)*
O = Observation *(special recall arranged)*
T = Treatment or investigation underway
R = Referred to any community or hospital service
N = Not examined for this item

Referred to (1) ____ (2) ____
(3) ____
Special recall in ____ wks/mths

Top Yellow Copy: DHA. 2nd Green Copy: to GP/HV
Third White Copy: stay in PCHR

13

Signature ____

6–8 weeks review

FIGURE 6.15J

Preschool/ School entry

Review at 4½ - 5½ years

Have you any worries about your child's
- eyesight Yes/no/not sure - speech Yes/no/not sure
- hearing Yes/no/not sure - growth Yes/no/not sure

Does your child wear:
- glasses Yes/no
- hearing aid Yes/no

Has your child ever seen a specialist? Yes/no
If 'Yes' please say what for ____
Does your child have any long term health problems? Yes/no
If 'Yes' please say what ____

Please list any medicines including creams, ointments, mixtures, tablets, inhalers etc that your child is taking regularly at the moment.
1 ____ 2 ____
3 ____ 4 ____

Do any of these medicines need to be taken during school hours? Yes/no
If 'Yes' please say which ones
1 ____ 2 ____

Children cannot judge the speed of cars very well. It is dangerous for them to cross major roads alone until the age of twelve.

23

FIGURE 6.15K

School entry

Continued

Does your child have any problems which may affect schooling? Yes/no/not sure
If 'Yes' or 'not sure' please say what the problem is ____

Is your child clumsy? Yes/no/not sure

Is your child clean and dry during the day and night? Yes/no/not sure
If 'No' or 'not sure' please say what the problem is ____

Does your child wheeze or have a night cough? Yes/no/not sure
Do you have any worries about your child's health? Yes/no/not sure
If 'Yes' or 'not sure' please say what the problem is ____

Do you have any worries about your child's behaviour? Yes/no/not sure
If 'Yes' or 'not sure' please say what the problem is ____

Comments ____

Are your child's immunisations up to date including the preschool booster? Yes/no

24

■ THINKING ABOUT OBSERVING

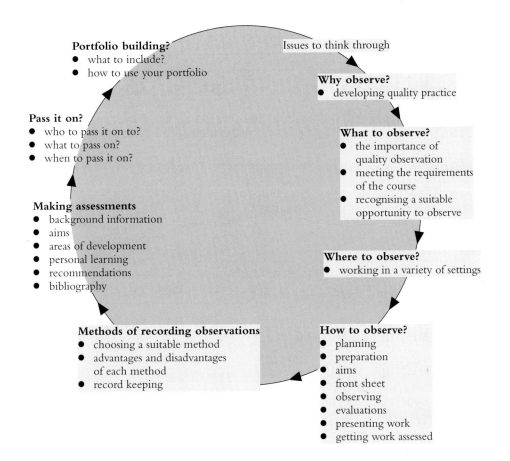

Portfolio building?
- what to include?
- how to use your portfolio

Issues to think through

Why observe?
- developing quality practice

Pass it on?
- who to pass it on to?
- what to pass on?
- when to pass it on?

What to observe?
- the importance of quality observation
- meeting the requirements of the course
- recognising a suitable opportunity to observe

Making assessments
- background information
- aims
- areas of development
- personal learning
- recommendations
- bibliography

Where to observe?
- working in a variety of settings

Methods of recording observations
- choosing a suitable method
- advantages and disadvantages of each method
- record keeping

How to observe?
- planning
- preparation
- aims
- front sheet
- observing
- evaluations
- presenting work
- getting work assessed

7

Making Assessments

Aims

The aims of this chapter are to:

- help you to make objective assessments
- help you to establish a format for assessments:

  1. *Background information.* Consider environmental factors which can influence the child's behaviour.

  2. *Your aims.* Look back at your aims frequently, to ensure you are working towards them.

  3. *Areas of development.* Assess the developmental progress of the child.

  4. *Recommendations.* Identify any practical ways in which your observations and

  assessments inform your practice through recommendations. Consider the recommendations made by others in the assessment process.

  5. *Personal learning.* Consider your own learning while carrying out your observation.

  6. *Bibliography.* Use the Harvard system.

- provide you with an example of a written assessment

- help you to evaluate and review any present format you might be using.

High quality assessment is an intellectual process of making judgements, drawing conclusions and making hypotheses based upon accurate, reliable observations and professional knowledge and expertise.

■ OBJECTIVITY

Now that you have completed the front sheet and main body of the observation, you need to think about making sense of what you have recorded so far. Bear in mind that your observations and subsequent assessments may be shared with other members of the team, other professionals, the child's parents or carers and the child. So ask yourself these questions:

- is it positive, highlighting strengths rather than weaknesses?
- does it describe the child's main activities, or does it sidetrack?

■ THE FORMAT

Your tutor or assessor might talk to you about how he/she would like you to write up the assessment. Sometimes this 'write up' is called a conclusion or an evaluation. Different courses will have particular requirements and the level of analysis needed will vary. It is important to discuss these requirements with your tutor or assessor. The following headings are likely to be used in some way or another, but don't follow this pattern rigidly, just dip in and out as the need arises.

1. *Background information*

You might like to include this section for setting the scene.
    You can ask yourself the following questions:

- What happened just before the observation took place?
- What is the weather like? (Sometimes the weather can affect the child's behaviour.)
- What is the child's cultural background?
- Is the child unwell?
- Does the child have special needs?
- Has anything of significance just happened in the child's life? (Check that this information is not confidential before noting it yourself.)

2. *Your aims*

Ask yourself 'did I achieve my aims?' If you did, did not, or did in part, then this is the first comment to make. For example, 'I achieved my aims in part by observing J's fine motor skills and problem-solving ability whilst playing with a jigsaw puzzle.'

3. *Areas of development*

Many observations require analysis of a child's developmental progress. The following sub-heading may help you with this.

Physical development

Look back at the main body of the observation for any evidence of:

- fine motor skills
- gross motor skills.

Now use this information to help you make an assessment. Refer to at least two textbooks and see what they say about physical development. With this information you have a basis for making an assessment of what you have observed.

Cognitive development

You can now follow the same process of using relevant information from the main body to help you make an assessment. Use your textbooks with reference to cognitive development.

Under this heading of cognitive development look particularly for examples of:

- imagination
- creativity
- language
- concentration
- purposeful action
- problem solving.

Emotional development

Follow the same process of using relevant information from the main body and referencing from your textbooks.

Under emotional development look particularly for examples of:

- use of non-verbal indicators such as facial expressions and body language generally
- use of verbal indicators such as crying and laughing.

Social development

You can now adopt the same process of using information from the main body and referencing from your textbooks.

Under social development look particularly for examples of:

- interaction between children
- interaction between children and adults
- emerging independence and self-help skills.
- reluctance to interact with others.

Now that you have considered these areas of development, look back at your aim. Were you looking for anything else that has not been covered so far? Perhaps you were asked to note how an adult deals with a distressed child. You could give yourself another heading and address that question specifically.

4. Recommendations

Once you have evaluated an observation you should be able to make recommendations to improve the quality of child care practice. You could try asking yourself these questions:

- Do I now need to provide anything extra for this child as a result of my assessments?
- Could I recommend any particular activities for this child?
- Have I identified any area of difficulty that may need help from another professional?
- Do I need to carry out another observation on this child, perhaps using another method of recording?
- Has any particular difficulty been identified as a result of the observation? (For example, is the child excessively tired?)
- Do I need to pass on any information to other members of the team or other adults?
- Do I need to change anything in my practice to ensure equality of opportunity?

5. *Personal learning*

Your evaluation should include a section on what you have personally learned from the observation. You could ask yourself these questions:

- Did anything surprise me?
- Did I learn anything in particular?
- Do I need to change anything in my practice as a result of this observation?
- Was this method of observing appropriate or would another method extract the information more easily?

Who can contribute to the assessment process?

Your placement supervisor may offer background information which will help you to make sense of what you have observed. There may have been some upheaval at home giving rise to a change in behaviour of the child. This information may be confidential so do check that you can include it in your assessment.

Sometimes the parent or carer may wish to contribute to the assessment particularly if you are working in a family placement. He/she might give you medical information or offer reasons for particular behaviour. Again do check that you can formally include the information.

The child may wish to comment or give his/her own view. The child's view is always important and forms a valuable part of the assessment process.

Assessment of a child's special needs

Your observations and assessments may be used as part of an overall assessment of a child's special educational need. Here, 'assessment' has a rather different meaning, specific to the particular context.

FIGURE 7.1A *Interaction between children*

FIGURE 7.1B *Interaction between children and adults*

Figure 7.1C *Musical activities help concentration*

Figure 7.1D *Sharing a book*

CHAPTER SEVEN *Activity*

Case Study

Aim: To help you plan observation work and to make assessments which enable positive progress for the child

You are working in a nursery.

Yasmin is 3 years old. She has just started nursery. She has a serious congenital heart defect which cannot yet be operated upon. She has been in hospital on a number of occasions. She gets very tired and breathless. Sometimes Yasmin can become quite aggressive towards her parents.

You would need to consult Yasmin's parents and plan some observation work.

- Which method would you use?
- What might Yasmin's needs be in the nursery?
- How might her social and emotional behaviour be affected by her congenital heart defect?

6. Bibliography

A bibliography could be your next heading. Most colleges prefer the Harvard system and this is how to record it:

- Surname of author(s) or editor
- Initials of author(s) or editor
- Date of edition
- Title
- Publisher
- Place of publication

The following is an example:

Bruce, T. & Meggitt, C. (1999) *Child Care and Education.* Hodder and Stoughton, London.

You should try to use several books to help with your assessments. This will give you a variety of viewpoints and help you link theory with practice. Your tutor or assessor will advise you about suitable up-to-date books.

Helpful hint

- Keep looking back at your aim to make sure that you are focused.
- Hand in your work on a regular basis for feedback.

■ EXAMPLE OF A STUDENT'S ASSESSMENT

The main body of this observation is given in Chapter 5 on page 42. Below is the assessment which follows. It was carried out during the student's first year of studying and is not intended to be a perfect example (if there is such a thing!) but is included here to give you a rough guide.

The aim

Assessment

To observe T while she plays on the school computer and to note her hand–eye co-ordination, concentration and interest in the programme.

I have achieved my aims through observing T whilst playing on the school computer.

Background information: T has just come in from playtime. It is a bright sunny day with little wind.

Physical development

I have found that T had very well-developed hand movements whilst using the computer keyboard. I also noticed that T demonstrated good hand–eye co-ordination.

When T was sitting on her stool she repeated forward and backward rocking movements.

Intellectual development

T showed good concentration through the computer program. Concentration was indicated by poking out her tongue. This concentration seemed to me to be an advantage to T as she succeeded in winning one of the mathematical computer puzzles which has to be solved in the game.

According to Lansdown and Walker (1991) T's concentration is normal for her age group:

'Children's ability to attend and maintain their attention usually increases markedly in all these dimensions over the years from three to seven.'

It would appear that T was genuinely interested in the program.

I think that T showed a high standard of reading ability and comprehension from the sections she read aloud from the computer, for example T said 'All their food has been eaten.'

Emotional development

At the end of the observation T showed that she was happy by smiling. I felt that this happiness was due to her achievements in the mathematical puzzle. According to an article in *Child Education* in 1988, written by Greenside and Williams, entitled 'First Programs', children should be allowed to work on computers at their own pace.

Overall, I felt that T expressed a rather sensible and fairly independent approach whilst working on the computer. This is quite acceptable for a child of five years, according to Sheridan (1991). T is six years old: 'So I would expect her general behaviour to be more sensible, controlled and independent.'

Recommendations

I feel T should be offered other games within the network to enable her to expand her knowledge and keyboard skills. According to the article mentioned previously (Greenside and Williams), although the initial aim may be to familiarise the child with a computer it will soon become apparent that through the use of programs you can further the child's intellectual abilities. Such development is best achieved by an adult occasionally working alongside the child and becoming involved in discussions to encourage exploration of all areas of the problem before the child finally reaches his/her own solution.

Equal opportunities: I have noted over the week that all children have a turn on the computer.

I would also like to do another observation of T, using the same method in a few months' time to monitor progress.

Personal learning

From completing this observation I feel that I have become more aware of the importance of computers in the school environment. I have also learned a lot about T herself. For example, she is a very competent reader and aware of how to use a computer and is familiar with the keys on the keyboard. This method of observing was satisfactory.

Quality control

Always protect the interests of the child. If you are not sure whether you should include a piece of information, then simply don't!

Bibliography

Lansdown, R. & Walker, M. (1991) *Your Child's Development from Birth to Adolescence.* Frances Lincoln, London.
Lindon, J. (1990) *Child's Development, Birth to Eight Years.* National Children's Bureau, London.
Sheridan, M. (1991) *From Birth to Five Years.* Routledge, London.

CHAPTER SEVEN *Activity*

Objectivity test for making assessments

Aim: To help you assess your observations objectively

From the following statements choose the ones that are objective.

1. Children were playing outside. Susan fell down a lot.
   a) Susan does not run as well as the other children in her peer group.
   b) Susan is developmentally delayed because she does not run as well as the others.
2. Rosalee spilled some paint on her paper and smeared it on with her hands.
   a) Rosalee is a messy child.
   b) Rosalee enjoys exploring materials in her own way.
3. Graham ran around the room saying 'Zoom!', carrying a wooden plane he had made.

a) Graham seemed pleased with the plane he had made and showed excitement.

b) Graham is a noisy child who runs around too much.

4. Ali built a complex structure out of blocks. Before the teacher could see it, another child ran past and it fell down. Ali cried.

a) Ali is babyish.

b) Ali was pleased with his achievement and appeared to need his teacher's approval.

It is important to keep to the facts when making your assessments in order to avoid subjective remarks. Then you will need to research relevant books to check the child's stage of development or progress to ensure your perceptions are correct.

Developmental expectations

	Physical	Intellectual	Emotional	Social
1 year old				
18 months				
2 years				

CHAPTER SEVEN *Activity*

Developmental norms

Aim: To help you learn about developmental norms and to encourage you to build up a useful form of reference

Choose at least two textbooks on child development and complete the chart on page 87.

In-depth discussion

It is a good idea to select suitable headings for your assessments which truly reflect the curriculum in your workplace.

Any assessment format needs to be periodically evaluated. Ask yourself these questions:

- Are my assessments reflecting anti-discriminatory practice?
- Am I making assessments in a purely mechanical manner or do I write each assessment with a view to actively making any necessary changes to my practice?
- Do I give myself the opportunity to review and evaluate examples of other written records of observations and assessments?
- Do I update my formats for assessments?
- Is my chosen format reliable for all children?
- Is my chosen format sensitive to different cultures and heritage languages in my workplace?

■ 'THE STARTING POINT FOR ASSESSMENT SHOULD BE POSITIVE, WHAT CAN THE CHILD DO?'

Evaluate this statement after looking at the following photographs.

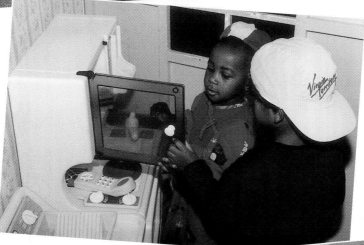

Summary

- Assessments need to take into account background information about factors which might influence a child's behaviour.
- Look at your aims when making your evaluation.
- When it is appropriate link to areas of development.
- Do you have any recommendations?
- Consider your personal learning.
- Ensure objectivity in your evaluations.

- Ask your tutor or assessor for any standard format he/she may require.
- Involve others in the assessment process.
- Use the example of an assessment process to help you.
- Use a range of textbooks about child developmental norms.
- Use the Harvard system for the Bibliography.
- Evaluate your assessment format.

■ THINKING ABOUT OBSERVING

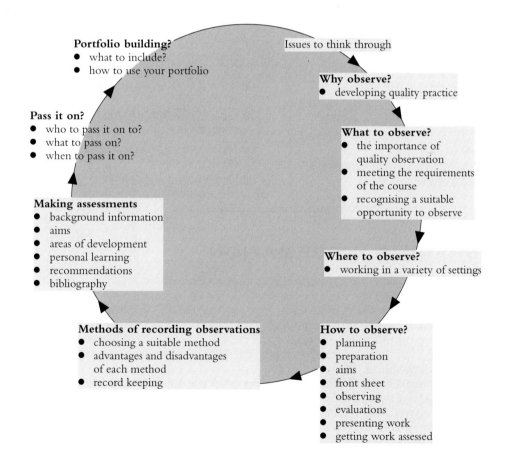

Portfolio building?
- what to include?
- how to use your portfolio

Pass it on?
- who to pass it on to?
- what to pass on?
- when to pass it on?

Making assessments
- background information
- aims
- areas of development
- personal learning
- recommendations
- bibliography

Methods of recording observations
- choosing a suitable method
- advantages and disadvantages of each method
- record keeping

Issues to think through

Why observe?
- developing quality practice

What to observe?
- the importance of quality observation
- meeting the requirements of the course
- recognising a suitable opportunity to observe

Where to observe?
- working in a variety of settings

How to observe?
- planning
- preparation
- aims
- front sheet
- observing
- evaluations
- presenting work
- getting work assessed

Pass it on?

Aims

This chapter aims to help you:

- appreciate the value of sharing information as a result of observation and assessment
- ensure that the rights of the child are not breached
- use specific guidelines for considering passing on information

- decide the appropriate audience for passing on information
- cultivate your skills in effective listening and communication
- decide what information is appropriate to pass on
- identify when it is appropriate to pass on information.

■ SHARING INFORMATION

Passing on information is an important part of the whole observation and assessment process.

If you are already working in an early years setting you will know that it is useful to share information with your colleagues. This process is often useful in checking whether pre-conceptions are influencing the early years workers' objective evaluation of observation. An open discussion between the workers who have observed should be of benefit to the child.

Early years workers need, therefore, to be good at learning from their observations in order to find out how to provide the best learning opportunities for a child.

The Children Act 1989 refers to the need for well-kept records as essential to good child protection practice. Each agency should have a policy which states the purpose and format of the records and the need to retain records for the appropriate amount of time. Information must be safeguarded and relevant records transferred when a child or family moves.

Quality control

Children have different learning styles and observing children at play can give valuable clues about how they process information for their own use. This information can be shared.

In-depth discussion

The learning styles of children can be quite individual. Think about five children in your care and consider their learning styles. Do they learn best by:

- being shown?
- being told?
- learning by making mistakes?
- working with other children?
- working alone?
- learning by experimentation?
- using their visual imagination?

Perhaps the children you have chosen are using a combination of the above. Now record your findings. Compare your findings with a partner.

When a child transfers to a reception class from a nursery, evidence gathered from observations can provide a building block from which the reception teacher, early years worker and other professionals can plan.

The rights of the child

When we pass on information we need to know that the interests of the child are being protected. We need to consider the rights of children and to ask questions of ourselves. For example, do children have a right to feedback from our observations?

The rights of the child are covered by the United Nations Conference, 1989, which identifies four broad themes of:

- survival
- development
- protection
- participation.

These themes emphasise the paramountcy of the child's welfare and the child's rights to:

- express views and be permitted freedom of expression, thought and association;
- be free from discrimination, inhumane treatment and unlawful restrictions of liberty;
- be free from all forms of sexual, physical and mental violence;
- information, education and health care.

The Children Act 1989, England and Wales, reflects a growing acceptance of children's rights.

In-depth discussion

Could there be a situation when the rights of the child conflict with the interests of the observer?

■ GUIDELINES

In most settings guidelines will exist about the passing on of information. Ask yourself, 'When I choose to pass on information will it . . .'

- affect the rights of the child?
- affect the rights of parents or carers?
- violate the principles of equal opportunities?
- support the child's cultural heritage and language?
- benefit the child?
- be specific and accurate?
- support the child's learning?
- support the child's development?
- be appropriate for the audience receiving it?

Whom to tell?

Keeping the above questions concerning guidelines in mind, we need to look at to whom we pass information. If you are in early years training, the first person to talk to is either your tutor or placement supervisor. Don't ever go straight to the parents/carers because you may only have half the story! It is as well to obtain as much advice as possible while you are still a student to prepare for when you have to take increased responsibility in decision making. Any situation or information which causes you concern should be fully discussed with your line manager, supervisor or tutor if you are a student.

Effective listening and receiving

Early years workers need to communicate well with children and adults. Communication starts with the ability to listen attentively.

Parents and carers, colleagues and other professionals may need to give you information regarding:

- the child's cultural and religious background
- relevant health factors
- any nervous habits
- who is collecting the child

- the child's preferred learning style
- the name by which the child is known
- information gathered from previous records.

Listen to the child

By listening to the child you will learn what the child thinks of you and the provision. You can trust the child to show you what he/she learns.

What to tell?

Look back at the questions concerning guidelines in this chapter to help you assess how you should respond to any information you are given. All personal information must be treated as confidential and you must use your integrity. Remember always to discuss any concerns you have with your supervisor, tutor or line manager.

Don't ever be tempted to discuss a child in a public place such as travelling home on a bus. That is breaching confidentiality.

Data protection

Your organisation will have its own guidelines drawn up. You must protect yourself and your organisation by making yourself familiar with these rules and adhering to them. When sharing information in a professional context try to avoid using jargon. Say what you mean in a way that can be clearly understood.

When to tell?

Again, look back at the questions concerning guidelines in this chapter and use them to assess when to pass on information.

However, you must be prepared to act upon what you see and hear in your work with children and to understand that by so doing you set events in motion. Acting on information gained is part of the work of child care and may result in further research, changes in practice and other consequences.

Child abuse

All workers with children have a duty to protect them from abuse. Work placements should have procedures for recording any signs of possible abuse.

Your observations of a child might lead you to suspect abuse, and in this case you would need to talk to your line manager, supervisor or tutor in confidence. Together you would decide the next step. The situation may require immediate referral, or it may not require urgent action and you will be advised to continue with your observation of the child.

Personal evaluation

It should help you to ask yourself what it is you are trying to do? You don't just want to rubber stamp your work, you need to evaluate and reflect.

In-depth discussion

It seems that early years workers need to meet to discuss their observations of children's learning. There needs to be some networking between provision.

a) Why might that be necessary?
b) How could that come about?
c) What benefits can you see?

CHAPTER EIGHT *Activity*

Passing on information

Aim: To learn about different audiences and to establish what others may or may not need to know

Preparation

Draw three columns. Take one of your observations and assessments and work on these three areas:

a) Make a list of all the people concerned with this child, for example, early years workers, parents/carers, specialists.
b) Now decide if there is anything each person might need to know about the child as a result of the observation.

Summary

- It is sometimes valuable to share information as a result of observation and assessment.
- Ensure that the rights of the child are not breached or ignored.
- Use the guidelines contained in this chapter when you are considering passing on the information.
- It is important to develop effective communication skills.

■ THINKING ABOUT OBSERVING

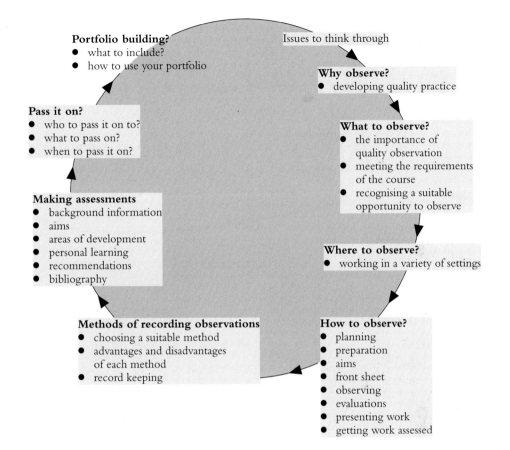

Portfolio building?
- what to include?
- how to use your portfolio

Issues to think through

Why observe?
- developing quality practice

Pass it on?
- who to pass it on to?
- what to pass on?
- when to pass it on?

What to observe?
- the importance of quality observation
- meeting the requirements of the course
- recognising a suitable opportunity to observe

Making assessments
- background information
- aims
- areas of development
- personal learning
- recommendations
- bibliography

Where to observe?
- working in a variety of settings

Methods of recording observations
- choosing a suitable method
- advantages and disadvantages of each method
- record keeping

How to observe?
- planning
- preparation
- aims
- front sheet
- observing
- evaluations
- presenting work
- getting work assessed

NINE

Portfolio Building for NVQ Assessment

Aims

The aims of this chapter are to explain:
- what a portfolio is
- the kind of things you include in a portfolio
- how to start building your portfolio
- how to use a portfolio.

■ WHAT IS A PORTFOLIO?

Quite simply, a portfolio is a collection of evidence about you and what you can do.

You may be very surprised at how much you have accomplished as you start collecting, in a folder, evidence of your achievements. For example, you may play a musical instrument to a certain grade; you may have a swimming certificate; GCSEs; a child care qualification; evidence of playing in a school football team; or voluntary work.

These types of achievements can all be included in your portfolio. A portfolio, as evidence of what you can do, is becoming increasingly important to employers when they appoint staff. It can also be important when applying for further education and training.

A portfolio is an integral part of every NVQ qualification and provides a major part of the evidence which supports your competence for assessment.

Assembling a portfolio is very worthwhile because it will increase your confidence as you identify all your achievements, and you will be able to use it to progress in your training or career. You can use it to gain employment, further education or training, and of course you can add all your subsequent achievements to your portfolio.

■ WHAT SHOULD BE INCLUDED IN A PORTFOLIO?

Apart from the things suggested above you can extend your description of yourself by, for example, saying 'I am calm in an emergency' and/or 'My hobbies include cycling', but don't make it too long.

All portfolios should include a curriculum vitae (CV) which summarises details about yourself and can be copied to any prospective employer or college/training establishment or voluntary body. If you have left school recently your Record of Achievement is your portfolio. Check that all the things you think should be in it are included.

Other useful items in a portfolio can include testimonials, photographs (for example of a display you worked on with children), certificates, etc.

Once you have completed your portfolio you can then consider what your aims are for the future as you see them at this point in your life. This will help you clarify what you need to do to achieve the goal you have set yourself in relation to your current completed portfolio.

■ BUILDING YOUR PORTFOLIO

The easiest starting point is your CV. Here is a list of what should be included:
Surname
    First name
    Previous surname(s)
Address and telephone number
Nationality
Date of birth
Name of secondary school
    Dates attended
    Examination results
Further Education and Training Course(s) undertaken
    Dates
    Results
    Qualifications and numbers if appropriate
Voluntary work
Employment (start at the top with current post)
    Give details of post, employer, type of job and dates.

End the CV with a general description about yourself and your particular hobbies and/or interests.

Leave space to include at least two referees and fill these in as appropriate for the post or course you are applying for. For example, your employment as a Saturday worker at a supermarket will not enable this employer to make a comment about your academic potential: your school or college is better able to do this.

Be prepared to talk about any aspect of your CV to an interviewer. It would be helpful to talk to someone who knows you well about the parts of your CV which may be particularly relevant to a post or a course. Those parts which are of particular relevance may need more space devoted to them, for example, if you're a lifeguard at present and you are applying to a job which involves taking children swimming. Your portfolio should contain evidence that you can do what you say you can.

The way you present your portfolio is important. It is worth taking time to buy a folder which is easy to open and shut, and to arrange the folder neatly, with an up-to-date contents page. The page shown below may be photocopied and placed at the front of your observation and assessment file.

■ HOW TO USE YOUR PORTFOLIO

Your portfolio has many uses. Here are some suggestions to help you.

- Always keep your portfolio ready for use.
- Make sure the information contained within it is up to date.
- For a job application for a college or training place your CV may be sufficient, but take your portfolio to an interview.
- Have your portfolio available and make sure you also have a copy of it.
- Always write a covering letter. Make this concise, and express your interest in the post.
- If you are offered the post or course/training reply promptly.
- If you are unsuccessful ask for some feedback: this could help you in the future.
- Make your portfolio a living document which you update and use selectively.
- Keep copies and file your portfolio in a safe place.

I certify that all the material contained in this observation and assessment file was undertaken at the time, date and place stated on each individual observation and assessment.

Signed
....

Candidate Registration No.
....

Centre No.
....

■ STAGES IN PRODUCTION OF A PORTFOLIO

1. Read through this guide.
2. Complete a CV.
3. Identify your sources of evidence.
4. Make a list of your evidence.
5. Collect all available evidence.
6. Add new evidence (if any).
7. Collate your portfolio.
8. Cross-reference your portfolio.
9. Keep your portfolio safe.

Summary

- ■ Your portfolio is about you and what you can do.
- ■ Your portfolio contains proof about what you can do.

- ■ Your portfolio can be added to as you gain further achievements.
- ■ Use your portfolio to help you progress in your career, your education and your training.

Further Reading

The National Diploma in Childhood Studies (Nursery Nursing), BTEC Publication No. 091445, London.

Bartholomew, L. and Bruce, T. (1993) *Getting to Know You: A guide to record keeping in early childhood education and care*. Hodder and Stoughton, London.

Bee, H. (1981) *The Developing Child*. Harper International, New York.

Berryman, J.C. (1991) *Developmental Psychology and You*. British Psychological Society and Routledge, London.

C.A.C.H.E. (1994) *The Overview Document NNEB Diploma in Nursery Nursing*.

Cambridge NEC Trust (1995) *NEC Children First*.

Drummond, M.J. (1993) *Assessing Children's Learning*. David Fulton, London.

Drummond, M.J., Rouse, D. and Pugh, G. (1992) *Making Assessment Work: Values and principles in assessing young children's learning*.

Harding, J. and Meldon–Smith, L. (2000) *Helping Young Children to Develop* 2nd Edition. Hodder & Stoughton, London.

HMSO (1991) *Working Together Under the Children Act, 1989*. HMSO, London.

HMSO (1994) *The National Occupational Standards for Early Years Care and Education*. Revised Standards (1997). Available from Awarding Bodies. 2nd edition. Local Government Board.

Hobart, C. & Frankel, J. (1994) *A Practical Guide to Child Observation*. Stanley Thornes, Cheltenham.

Laishley, J. (1987) *Working with Young Children*. Hodder and Stoughton, London.

Lindon, J. and L. (1993) *Caring for the Under-8s, Working to active good practice*. Macmillan, London.

Nutbrown, C. (1994) *Threads of Thinking, Young Children learning and the role of early education*. Paul Chapman Publishing Ltd, London.

O'Hagan, M. & Smith, M. (1993) *Special Issues in Child Care*. Bailliere Tindall, London.

Pre-School Learning Alliance (1991) *Equal Chances: Eliminating discrimination and ensuring equality in play groups*. PSLA, London.

Pugh, G. (ed.) (1992) *Contemporary Issues in Early Years, working collaboratively for children*. Paul Chapman Publishing, London.

Sheridan, M. (1999) *Play in Early Childhood – From Birth to Six Years*. Routledge, Cornwall.

Sylva, K. & Painter, M. (1980) *Childwatching at Playgroup and Nursery School*. Grant McIntyre, London.

Webb, L. (1981) *Making a start on Child Study*. Basil Blackwell, Oxford.

Williams, K. & Gardner, R. (1993) *Caring for Children*. Pitman Publishing, London.

Wolfendale, S. (1990) *All About Me*. WGS Arnold, Nottingham.